Discipline and Critique

D1572720

SUNY Series in Contemporary Continental Philosophy
Dennis J. Schmidt, Editor

Discipline and Critique

*Kant, Poststructuralism, and
the Problem of Resistance*

Andrew Cutrofello

State University of New York Press

Published by
State University of New York Press, Albany

For information, address State University of New York
Press, State University Plaza, Albany, N.Y. 12246.

Production by E. Moore
Marketing by Bernadette LaManna

Library of Congress Cataloging-in-Publication Data

Cutrofello, Andrew, 1961-
    Discipline and critique : Kant, poststructuralism, and
the problem of resistance / Andrew Cutrofello
        p. cm.— (SUNY series in contemporary continental
philosophy)
    Includes bibliographical references and index.
    ISBN 0-7914-1855-3 (hard : alk. paper).—ISBN 0-7914-1856-1
(pbk. : alk. paper)
    1. Kant, Immanuel, 1724-1804. 2. Postmodernism. I. Title.
II. Series.
B2798.C88 1994   93-3843
193—dc20   CIP

10 9 8 7 6 5 4 3 2 1

Contents

Acknowledgments

Martin Donougho, Tamsin Lorraine, and Cynthia Willett each read a complete draft of this book. Their discerning judgment and generous criticisms helped make *Discipline and Critique* a considerably better work than it could otherwise have been.

Mary Caputi, Ann K. Clark, and Alan Rosiene each read drafts of individual chapters and gave me the benefit of their always keen insights. Conversations with them have also enabled me to strengthen a number of specific arguments. In addition, I am grateful for discussions with the students at Saint Mary's College who took my "Kant and his Critics" course in the spring of 1992.

With Alison Leigh Brown I have discussed a good many of the ideas that come up in this book. Her influence is especially evident in chapter 8. I am also grateful for helpful discussions with Craig Hanks, David Ingram, Kathleen League, Bill Martin, Kelly Oliver, and John Wright.

Karl Ameriks, Anthony Cascardi, John McCumber, Charlene Haddock Seigfried, and Patrick E. White offered much-appreciated encouragement on this project. Margaret Nash suggested the possibility of a homoerotic reading of the relationship between Kant and Lampe.

In January 1993, I presented an overview of the book to members of the Philosophy department at the University of Colorado at Denver. Soonok Choi, Sharon Coggan, Georg Gadow, Honi Haber, Glenn Webster, and Mark Yarborough offered valuable suggestions, and they showed me where I needed to improve the exposition of my arguments.

A much earlier draft of chapter 2 was presented at the Popular Culture Association conference in Louisville, Kentucky, in March 1992. An earlier draft of chapter 4 was presented at the "Persons, Passions, Powers" conference at the University of California at Berkeley in May 1992. My participation at this conference was supported through a Lilly Endowment faculty development grant. I am grateful for the comments I received at these talks.

Clay Morgan has been a terrific editor. Thanks to Peg Shiro and Elizabeth Moore for additional editorial support. I would also like to acknowledge my gratitude to Dennis Schmidt for including *Discipline and Critique* in his series on Contemporary Continental Philosophy.

I dedicate this book to Dianne Rothleder, who also read a complete draft and recommended improvements. To her example of philosophical creativity, I have aspired. And of course many special thanks to Megan Rose, our daughter. Among other things, she let me play with her blocks. Finally, open-ended thanks to my parents, Paul and Rita Carroll Cutrofello and the rest of my family.

It is my hope that the reader will credit those mentioned here for anything that might be found to be worthwhile in this book. Whatever faults there are should of course, be blamed solely on the author.

Preface

In this book, I plan to recast Kantian philosophy along poststructuralist lines. In particular, I show how Kantian ethics can be reformulated in a way that takes into account criticisms that have been articulated by Foucault, Lacan, Deleuze, Guattari, Irigaray, Derrida, and others.

Schematically, my work can be seen as intervening in the debate that continues to take place between modernists and poststructuralists concerning the possibility—or desirability—of an ethical theory. At the heart of this debate is a question of what it means to engage in critique.

For Kant, critique is a juridical-style questioning of the claims of reason which seeks to establish universal standards of rationality. Kant's modernist heirs accept this basic model, although with important modifications.

In Habermas, the Kantian tribunal is transformed into a public court governed by democratic procedures which are designed to let all rational agents participate in its deliberations. However the Habermasian court retains the basic Kantian framework of critique as some sort of juridically styled questioning. The trope of the *court* is meant to conjure the ideal of a common space for rendering differences commensurable in accordance with regulative assumptions about universal rationality.

Poststructuralists, by contrast, reject—or at least problematize—the very idea of a critical court of reason because they question the assumption that differences can be "settled" in a court with universalist pretensions. Both Lyotard's notion of the "differend" and Derrida's conception of "the aporias of justice," for instance, would undermine the foundations upon which a critical court of reason would stake its claim to legitimacy. In calling into question the juridical model of critique, poststructuralists not only cast suspicion on the Enlightenment project, but they also raise doubts about the possibility of a non-coercive normative theory. The basis for these doubts can be traced to the work of Foucault.

There is still considerable disagreement among Foucault's interpreters about where he stood with respect to the so-called project of modernity. This situation is complicated by the fact that, throughout his career, Foucault was continually reworking his own methods of inquiry. Much of the recent literature on Foucault is concerned with deciding whether Foucault should be thought of as working within the Enlightenment tradition or outside of it—a dilemma which continues despite the fact that (or perhaps because) Foucault himself refused the alternatives. David Couzens Hoy suggests that "the dispute between Habermas and Foucault turns on whether Foucault is understood to be criticizing modernity from a postmodern or a premodern perspective."[1]

To an extent Hoy is right, but this either/or set of alternatives—premodern/postmodern, for/against modernity—threatens to eclipse what seems to have been unique in Foucault's thought. My thesis is that Foucault's entire career was a sustained attempt to formulate a nonjuridical model for Kantian critique, and that—in groping towards such a model—he was led to think with modernity against modernity. However, despite his advances in this direction, Foucault remained uncertain about whether he meant to put forth a general ethical theory. As some of his critics have argued, Foucault frequently seems to invoke an imperative to resist all forces of domination. Yet at the same time he suggests that any practical imperatives are themselves instruments of domination. How to specify a Foucauldian practical ethic is a problem which many of his followers have been working on since his death. My aim in this book is to construct a Foucauldian ethic using genealogically critiqued—that is, nonjuridical—Kantian tools.

Exactly what it means to presuppose a juridical model of critique is a question which Kant himself never fully formulated. He fashioned his critical court of reason at a time when European courts were being transformed into instruments of disciplinary power, and we can see the Kantian court mimetically reproducing some of these effects. The concept of discipline, in fact, plays a central role in Kantian critique, and I will show how this concept relates to the Foucauldian understanding of disciplinary power.

Unlike Foucault, Kant attempted to distinguish between two different types of discipline. He recognized a discipline of domination which correlates to the Foucauldian conception of discipline, but he also called attention to the possibility of what I call a "discipline of resistance". Retrieving the Kantian ideal of a discipline of resistance I will argue can provide the basis for the kind of Foucauldian ethic which Foucault himself never formulated. However, to the extent that Kant was unable to radically question his juridical model, he was unable to distinguish adequately between a discipline of resistance and a discipline of domination. My aim will be to show where Kant goes wrong, and to try to recover the resources he provides for thinking through the possibility of a discipline of resistance. My fear is that Habermas' Kantianism has further buried—rather than retrieved—these resources.

While my attempt to trace the role of discipline in Kant's philosophy will focus on his texts, it is impossible to read Kant's doctrine of practical discipline without calling attention to the way in which he applied this doctrine to his own life. An analysis of Kant's disciplinary "care of the self" will be called upon in chapters 4 and 7 in order to shed light on the practical consequences of his regimented program. While the burden of my arguments will rest on an analysis of Kant's philosophical claims, a genealogical reading of his texts requires that we look at his life as well.

Chapter One

The Search for a Metadeduction of the Juridical Model of Critique

In the *Critique of Pure Reason*, Kant puts reason on trial, at the same time giving to reason the right to judge itself. Kant's idea of the "tribunal of reason" must be understood in this double sense: reason stands before the court of reason. What summons this court, Kant suggests, is the present historical age itself.

> It is obviously the effect not of levity but of the matured judgment of the age, which refuses to be any longer put off with illusory knowledge. It is a call to reason to undertake anew the most difficult of all its tasks, namely, that of self-knowledge, and to institute a tribunal which will assure to reason its lawful claims, and dismiss all groundless pretensions, not by despotic decrees, but in accordance with its own eternal and unalterable laws. This tribunal is no other than the *critique of pure reason*.[1]

To be sure, Kant is not the first philosopher to view philosophical questioning in juridical terms. The tradition goes back at least as far as Aristotle, whose *categoria* are—as Kant himself reminds us—legal accusations. However there is something about the present age, Kant suggests, that calls forth a tribunal of reason. The present age's resolve to put itself on trial is a mark of its "matured judgment . . . Our age is, in especial degree, the age of criticism [*Kritik*], and to criticism everything must submit."[2]

In this passage, the word *Kritik* has a slight—but importantly—broader sense than did the sense given to it

1

in the title of Kant's work. Kant insists that a critique of reason must be complete. Were a single claim of reason exempted from examination, the trial would have to be declared a mistrial. However, there are two different types of completeness. One corresponds to the broader, and the other to the narrower senses of critique.

In the wider sense, the trial of reason should examine all of the principles of reason, plus all of the derivative concepts that can be generated on the basis of these principles. However, the trial can be divided into a two-step process. First the principles can be put before the tribunal of reason. Later, the derivative concepts can appear before the court.

Kant pledges to undertake only the first of these two steps. Both taken together constitute critique in the broader sense of transcendental philosophy. To his own project of undertaking a complete examination of the fundamental principles of reason, Kant gives *critique* the narrower sense of, as his book is titled, *Critique of Pure Reason*.

Completeness for this first *Critique* is, therefore, narrower than the completeness required by transcendental philosophy. For the present work, Kant states, it will be sufficient to "provide a complete enumeration of all the fundamental concepts that go to constitute . . . pure knowledge." It is not necessary to provide an "exhaustive analysis of the whole of *a priori* human knowledge."[3] Were we were to wonder whether the lack of completeness in the broader sense might be grounds for mistrial in the first *Critique*, Kant assures us of the separateness of the two cases. Laying out the principles of reason is its own task, the results of which do not depend in any way on how we think about the concepts which we will derive from our investigation. Moreover, because the ground for derivative concepts is provided by the *Critique* itself, we can rest assured that the second stage of the trial will not introduce any "surprise witness" who might provide evidence that would require us to declare the first stage to be invalid. That the "trial of the derivatives" is less important than and irrelevant to the "trial of the principles" is expressed by Kant in his claims that all of the serious work of transcendental philosophy will have been completed with the *Critique* itself. Hence, the task of providing the sort of exhaustive analysis which transcendental philosophy calls for is described as "rather an amusement than a labour,"[4] and as something "easily performed."[5] Clearly, Kant anticipates no "surprise witnesses."

The distinction between a "complete enumeration" and an "exhaustive analysis" appears in the Transcendental Analytic of the first *Critique*, in which Kant provides the tables of judgments and categories in a way that is famous for its suddenness and lack of argument. In the tables, Kant clearly feels that enumeration is more important than analysis. Hence, he defers any discussion of the equally pure predicables which can be derived from the categories themselves. When he turns to the task of providing a deduction of the categories, Kant does not raise the question of whether the predicables might, themselves, require a separate sort of deduction. After all, if the predicables are merely derivative concepts analytically implied by the categories, then a deduction of the latter should amount to a deduction of the former as well.

However, what if it should turn out that reason is capable of producing types of judgments that differ from the sort of categorical judgments that are put before the tribunal in the first *Critique*? To be complete, transcendental philosophy must question the legitimacy of every distinctive type of utterance which we make. If a type of judgment were discovered which was not covered by the table of judgments, then a separate deduction of its claims would need to be provided. In a similar vein, mathematical judgments, the legitimate application of which to experience is demonstrated in the *Critique's* Transcendental Aesthetic, require a separate deduction, one which Kant takes to have been provided in the Transcendental Aesthetic.[6]

Were we to discover any type of utterance, the legitimacy of which we had not questioned, the completeness criterion of transcendental philosophy would require us to attempt a deduction of its claims by examining the origin of its concepts. It was a similar discovery that led Kant to formulate the plan of the *Critique of Judgment*. Originally, he had thought that all judgments were either theoretical or practical, and, therefore, that the critiques of pure and practical reason would exhaustively question the legitimacy of the types of things we say. Then Kant came to believe that aesthetic and teleological judgments were different sorts of utterances, neither theoretical nor practical. Each required a separate critique of its own, and, thus, the two-fold plan of a third critique was formed.

The critique of aesthetic judgment introduces the sort of "surprise witnesses" that Kant thought he didn't have to worry about. The concepts of the beautiful and the sublime are precisely the sort of derivative concepts that the first *Critique* had put to one side. An object that appears beautiful, for instance, is one that cannot be rendered fully determinate by the categories of the understanding. Judging an object to be beautiful involves a use of our faculties that the first *Critique* had claimed to be impossible. Kant—as many critics have pointed out—fails to see the extent to which his analysis of aesthetic judgments problematizes the claim of the first *Critique* to demonstrate that all experiences must be adequately subsumable under the categories. However, Kant continued to believe that the trial of pure principles was complete.

Should Kant have written a third edition of the *Critique of Pure Reason*? Or does his analysis of aesthetic judgments somehow call into question the critical project itself? According to Kant, the integrity of his project depends upon its completeness. But is it capable of completion? To judge an object to be beautiful, Kant suggests, is to recognize that the object occasions an endless process of reflection. The more we look at something that is beautiful, the more we have to say about it. This process involves not only the continual application of concepts which we already possess, but also the creation of new concepts. The more we look at a beautiful work of art, for instance, the more we grope for new words to characterize what we experience in it. Now, do these new words represent mere *empirical* concepts? Or do they function as new *categories*? Obviously, Kant does not countenance the latter possibility. However, on his own account, aesthetic experience arises from a breakdown of the understanding. The concepts which we invent to characterize a beautiful object function, as it were, in the place of the categories. To be sure, none of the concepts we invent are ultimately capable of completely determining the object which we call beautiful, but this says only that they possess the same defect as do the categories themselves.

If we take seriously the sorts of problems that the *Critique of Judgment* poses for transcendental philosophy, what we come up against is the demand for a perpetual deduction of new categories. It was Hegel who took seriously the view that reflection occasions the invention of new categories. The *Phenomenology of Spirit* recounts this process, and the *Science of Logic* explicates the categories themselves. In recognizing that reflection gives rise, not just to new empirical concepts but also to new categories of thought, Hegel realized (as he explains in the famous preface to the *Phenomenology*) the inadequacy of the Kantian approach to a critique of knowledge. Kant, of course, does not make this move because it would require him to abandon his claim to have discovered a finite set of a priori categories that are determinately—rather than reflectively—applicable to experience.

For this reason, Kant took the task of providing a complete transcendental deduction of the categories to be central to the success of his critical enterprise. The burdens of the transcendental deduction in the first *Critique* are several. The deduction must show, first, that the categories are a priori and not derived from experience. Second, the deduction must determine the source of the categories. Third, the deduction must establish the objective validity of applying the categories to experience.

All of these tasks are essentially linked to the juridical element of Kantian critique. The burden of a deduction is to establish the *quid juris* of the use of concepts which we use in making particular types of judgment. Kant borrows the phrase *quid juris* from the language of the courts. The aim of the *Deduktionsschriften* was, as Dieter Henrich points out, "to justify controversial legal claims."[7] In Kant's day, jurists would submit a deduction in cases in which a claim of entitlement was under dispute. "Not only is the argumentation of the deduction correlative to the juridical argumentative form . . ., the text of the transcendental deduction is a deduction writing in the technical sense."[8] The *quid juris* which Kant seeks to establish in the Transcendental Deduction of the first *Critique* is, precisely, a decision regarding a question concerning the "legal entitlement" of the categories. As an attempt to question the legitimacy of a certain claim, a deduction can be thought of only in juridical terms.[9]

In Kant's view, the entire critique of reason must be juridical because reason itself is inherently juridical, acting like a court even when it is not engaged in critique. Gillian Rose calls attention to this fact, characterizing the invitation to critique as an invitation to witness a court that is always already in session.

> Today things will be slightly different. You are on trial. Or, rather, you are to be invited to inspect a court-room in which you have been judge, witness, and clerk for so long that you have ceased to notice its strange *ambience*.[10]

That reason has these juridical roles to perform—that reason is always already "in session"—is a basic assumption of Kant's enterprise. The aim of critical philosophy is to help reason perform its various juridical roles more conscientiously.

The most important aim of the first *Critique* is to distinguish between a dogmatic court of reason and a critical court of reason. The tribunal of critical reason functions as a sort of appeals court that must review the decisions of the lower court. This lower court, it turns out, tends to issue judgments that are based on a merely partial assessment of the evidence. All of its metaphysical decisions are of this sort. The critical court is fairer because it is more scrupulous. When it determines that rival claimants have had equally good evidence in support of their respective claims, the higher court suspends the judgments of the lower court. If critical reason, as a judge, fails to settle these cases with a new decision, it is not because it shirks its juridical responsibility but precisely because it performs its juridical functions more conscientiously than does dogmatic reason.

The juridical model of Kant's court of reason is not merely a rhetorically useful way of characterizing a certain mode of questioning. It is, in an important way, the essence of that mode of questioning. Because critique is inherently juridical, it should also be no surprise that the tribunal of reason may be incapable of radically questioning its own juridical status. The trial of reason may be reflexive with respect to reason—that is, reason can question reason—but it is not reflexive with respect to the tribunal itself. Because the Kantian tribunal can only raise juridical questions, it could question itself only by putting itself on trial—either by somehow appearing before itself, or perhaps by submitting its claims before a still higher, more critical court of reason. Either way, this could result only in a form of self-justification that would seem to be viciously circular. The court of critical reason can question the authority of the court of dogmatic reason, but it does not seem capable of radically questioning the legitimacy of its juridical character as such.

Whether or not Kantian critique does possess the resources to question the legitimacy of its own juridical model, critique's demand for completeness should require such a questioning. The juridical model of critique should stand in need of some sort of deduction, because the deductions themselves rest on an assumption about the a priori legitimacy of this model. In other words, the idea of a juridical deduction appears to be a kind of transcendental concept that is more fundamental for the deductions than even the transcendental unity of apperception. Should we not therefore expect Kantian critique to provide a deduction of its own juridical model? Right away, the form of this question traps us. To ask for the *quid juris* of the tribunal of reason itself would simply be to raise another juridical question.

What we are looking for is a way of undertaking a metadeduction of the juridical model of critique that would not itself be juridically modeled. However, is this undertaking doomed from the first? The difficulty is that all the tools of critique are themselves juridical. The very word *metadeduction* continues to invoke the juridical.

The problem posed here is a variant on a theme. The more general problem of how to subject critique to critique is an old one and is associated with the project of metacritique—a project that goes back to Kant's contemporary critics, Herder and Hamann. The burden of a metacritique is to radicalize the critical project by submitting its own presuppositions to critique. Garbis Kortian describes the problem as follows:

> How can [a] presupposition which supports the critical enterprise be brought to light? A "critique of critique" will not suffice. This would simply involve the contradictory demand that critique, ignorant of the dimension which makes critique possible, should make good its own defect. Hence metacritique. . . . Metacritique is true critique, or rather, it is what critique becomes when it is made radical. The critique of knowledge is limited by the fact that there is always something which it does not criticise. It does not criticise itself, in other words, its initial conception of what knowledge is.[11]

The distinguishing mark of metacritique is its rejection of the Kantian assumption that the project of critique has a kind of a priori legitimacy. In the words of Jürgen Habermas, the foremost proponent of the metacritical tradition today, "The only thing standing at the beginning of critique is the radical project of unconditional doubt. From Descartes to Kant this doubt required no justification because it legitimated itself as an aspect of reason."[12] It is Hegel who effectively challenges this presupposition.

> Hegel radicalizes the approach of the critique of knowledge by subjecting its presuppositions to self-criticism. In so doing he destroys the secure

foundation of transcendental consciousness, from which the a priori demarcation between transcendental and empirical determinations, between genesis and validity, seemed certain.[13]

Hegelian phenomenology traces the historical processes by which structures of consciousness are generated. What appeared to Kant to be a priori conditions for the possibility of experience turn out to be dialectically constituted structures of historical experience. However, from Habermas's perspective, Hegel's metacritique did not go far enough in questioning the historical character of consciousness because he himself presupposed key assumptions of the Schellingian philosophy of identity. As a result, Hegel was unable to understand how the historical structures of consciousness developed from—and in opposition to—the material structures of the social world. Hence, the Hegelian metacritique had to be supplemented with a metacritique of it, which Habermas takes Marx to have provided.

> In opposition to Hegel's position in the *Phenomenology* Marx holds the conviction that the self-reflection of consciousness discloses the fundamental structures of social labor, discovering therein the synthesis of the objectively active natural being man and the nature that is his objective environment.[14]

Marx thereby opens up the possibility for a genuinely historical metacritical epistemology. However, because Marx accepted the Hegelian dismissal of epistemology, he himself failed to develop his own resources for a metacritical epistemology. Instead, he fell back on a dogmatic positivism. "Thus in Marx's works a peculiar disproportion arises between the practice of inquiry and the limited philosophical self-understanding of this inquiry."[15] Instead of developing "a really radicalized critique of knowledge," Marxist metacritique regresses to a precritical dogmatism which grants to scientific reason an authority unchecked by philosophical reflection.[16] Thereafter, arose the positivistic tradition that begins with Comte, and against which the Marxist tradition has little to say. After Marx, the metacritical tradition went largely into eclipse until the rise of neo-Kantianism and critical theory. Habermas sees himself as resurrecting this tradition.

There are certain ways in which Habermas questions the specific juridical character of Kantian critique. In his essay, "Philosophy as Stand-In (*Platzhalter*) and Interpreter," he seeks to distance himself from the "master-thinker" tradition which places the philosopher as the final judge of all intellectual matters. In Habermas' view, Kant both does and does not belong to this tradition. Kant is taken to be a master thinker to the extent that he took transcendental philosophy to establish epistemology as the arch-science, with the authority to judge the epistemic claims of all other domains of cognitive inquiry.

> What Kant calls "transcendental" is an inquiry into the a priori conditions of what makes experience possible. The specific upshot of Kant's transcendental inquiry is that those conditions are identical with the conditions of possible objects of experience. . . . As a master thinker, Kant fell into disfavor because he used transcendental justification to found the new discipline of epistemology. In so doing he redefined the task, or vocation if you like, of philosophy in a more demanding way.[17]

Habermas agrees with Kant's detractors in rejecting the claim that epistemology should play the role of the supreme judge of all of the other sciences (*Wissenschaften*).

> Kantian philosophy sets up a domain between itself and the sciences, arrogating authority to itself. It wants to clarify the foundations of the sciences once and for all, defining the limits of what can and cannot be experienced. This is tantamount to an act of ushering the sciences to their proper place. I think philosophy cannot and should not try to play the role of usher.[18]

Moreover, because Kant takes epistemology to be capable of legislating for all spheres of activity over and beyond the merely cognitive-instrumental, transcendental philosophy is set up as "the highest court of appeal vis-a-vis the sciences and culture as a whole."[19]

Although he rejects the view that the philosopher should play the role of judge, Habermas does not reject the a priori legitimacy of the juridical model of Kantian critique. For Habermas, critique is essentially juridical. It requires a court before which competing claims are to be heard, and, for this, the role of judge remains indispensable. What Habermas challenges is simply the Kantian assumption that it is the *philosopher* who is entitled to play the role of judge. Essentially a liberal reformer of the court rather than a radical challenger to it, Habermas seeks a revised critical legal system with a new sort of judge presiding over a new court of reason. The specific reforms that Habermas introduces parallel the types of liberal reforms that have been developed in democratic legal systems. In place of the absolute monarchy of the philosopher-judge that we find in Kant, Habermas seeks to articulate the conditions under which the equally sovereign members of a democratic society could collectively preside over the court of reason. What this amounts to is the construction of a procedural legalistic model, whose conclusions regarding the claims of reason will not require the absolutist character that Kant's foundationalist court would demand.

With his procedural court in place, Habermas can argue against the view, expressed by Rorty, that "without the Kantian assumption that the philosopher can decide *questiones juris* concerning the rest of culture," we must reject the role of the philosopher as "guardian of rationality."[20] For Habermas, the metacritical challenge is simply to reclaim the modernist "belief in procedural rationality."[21] Put otherwise, if the role of judge is no longer appropriate for the philosopher, the role of guardian of the court still remains. Because he remains committed to the juridical model of Kantian critique, Habermas' *metacritique* cannot provide a *metadeduction* of the juridical model of critique.

In *Knowledge and Human Interests*, Habermas notes that the debate which characterizes the modern period can be characterized as a judicial hearing: "If we imagine the philosophical discussion of the modern period reconstructed as a judicial hearing, it would be deciding a single question: how is reliable knowledge (*Erkenntnis*) possible?"[22] The later theory of communicative action calls, in effect, for a new trial with a new charge. The claims of reason must now meet with the consensus of rational agents who have conducted an open, noncoercive discussion. As Kortian further notes, it is precisely here that we see Habermas' "return to the *quaestio quid juris*"[23]. "The meaning given to validity (*Geltung*) in response to the Kantian question of right establishes *a kind of tribunal* of discursive argumentation before which rationality may be vindicated."[24]

Without the ability to raise the metadeductive question, can Habermas' metacritique really meet the metacritical challenge to submit all of the claims of reason to critique? As in Kant, the Habermasian court of reason—the community of rational agents—is willing to hear all appeals that are brought before it, except for one. The authority of the court itself cannot be challenged. All questions of legitimation must be brought before a court whose procedural model is, by definition, legitimated a priori. Habermas responds to criticisms of this sort by pointing out the ineluctability of some presupposed criterion of legitimation—that is, some juridical standard. In this way he resorts to his familiar charge of "performative contradiction" whenever anyone seeks to further radicalize the metacritical project. As Richard Bernstein puts it:

> Critique . . . must preserve at least one standard by which we engage in the critique of the present. Yet when critique is *totalized*, when critique turns against itself so that all rational standards are called into question, then one is caught in a performative contradiction.[25]

Without putting too much weight on biographical observations, we can speculate that Habermas' commitment to the juridical model of critique may have arisen from his early reflections on the Nuremberg trials.

> At the age of 15 or 16, I sat before the radio and experienced what was being discussed before the Nuremberg tribunal, when others, instead of being struck by the ghastliness, began to dispute the justice of the trial, procedural questions, and questions of jurisdiction.[26]

The question of the legitimacy of an international court seemed, to the young Habermas, to be of secondary import to the horror of the crimes of the accused, and much of his later work can be read as an attempt to specify the conditions that would legitimate an international court such as the one at Nuremberg. In his dispute with Gadamer over the degree to which individuals' capacity for judgment is limited by their particular cultures, Habermas is clearly motivated by his view that a strict Gadamerian line would preclude the possible legitimacy of a Nuremberg trial.

What lurks beneath Habermas's call for a procedural construction of universal standards of legitimacy is an a priori assumption about the legitimacy of such a project. What sanctions this project also is nothing less than the undeduced ideal of a court of reason. Thus, what motivates Habermas's commitment to the juridical model—and his refusal of the idea of a total critique that would call it into question—is a *petitio principi* that deduces the possibility of universalist standards of rationality from the ideal of a court whose legitimacy itself rests on that same possibility.

As did Kant, the only sort of questioning of the juridical model which Habermas can conceive of would be, precisely, a juridical critique of critique. All questioning must, itself, already be critique, so the questioning of critique is merely an extension of critique itself—a reflexive, self-destructing project in Habermas's view. Surely we can grant Habermas the selfdestructive character of a total critique without conceding that every questioning of juridical critique must, of itself, be a juridical questioning. Put otherwise, it remains to be seen whether it is possible to question the court of reason in a way that takes place out of court without, thereby, being susceptible to the *charge* of being out of court. To the extent that Habermas charges every mode of questioning with presenting a juridical case before the court of reason, his court—despite its supposedly democratic and procedural character—is just as absolutist as the Kantian court. Yet the challenge which Habermas poses is, nonetheless, a formidable one. Is it possible to question the juridical model of critique in a way that will not require us to submit a petition before the court of reason?

The problem is to determine how we can undertake a metadeduction of the juridical model of critique without presupposing as Habermas insists we will some juridically modeled legitimation claims. Obviously, the word *metadeduction* retains a linguistic tie to the juridical. But this does not mean that a metadeduction must mimic the juridical form of a Kantian deduction. The etymology shows, however, that critique itself both requires and resists the sort of radical questioning which a metadeduction would undertake. A metadeduction is yet is not a deduction. We cannot question the court of reason's claim to authority by inquiring into the *quid juris* in something like "the case of the tribunal of reason." Yet, neither can we lapse into a nonphilosophical questioning of the court of reason. We must resist falling into both the Scylla of the juridical and the Charybdis of the nonphilosophical. Within the metacritical tradition itself, there have been at least two important attempts at a nonjuridical questioning of the claims of reason—those undertaken by Hegel and by Heidegger. Both, however, ultimately fail to directly question the juridical as such.

As Habermas reminds us, Hegelian phenomenology criticizes the Kantian pretense that critique can yield a kind of "knowing before knowledge."

> The critical philosophy (*Kritizismus*) demands that the knowing subject ascertain the conditions of the knowledge of which it is in principle capable before trusting its directly acquired cognitions. Only on the basis of reliable criteria of the validity of our judgments can we determine whether we may also

be certain with regard to our knowledge. But if this critique itself must claim to be knowledge, how can we critically investigate the cognitive faculty prior to knowing?[27]

In dismissing critical philosophy's claim to discern a priori standards of validity, Hegel, in effect, rejects Kant's a priori invocation of a legitimate and legitimating court of reason. Instead of beginning by calling such a court into session, Hegelian phenomenology will inquire into the social formations which generate standards of legitimation.

However, what Hegel promises is not what he delivers. In fact, Hegel himself presupposes a kind of legitimacy for the final result of his phenomenological inquiry, the telos which informs all of the legitimation claims of the *Phenomenology*. This telos is that legitimated and legitimating standard of absolute knowledge which "we," as phenomenological observers, always already possess. As Habermas observes, this a priori claim to a standard of legitimation— the identity of subject and object—is revealed in the relationship between phenomenology and systematic philosophy in Hegel—a relationship which basically recapitulates the Kantian claim to a "knowing before knowing."

> If it is phenomenology that first produces the standpoint of absolute knowledge, and this standpoint coincides with the position of authentic scientific knowledge, then the construction of knowledge in its manifestations cannot itself claim the status of scientific knowledge. The apparent dilemma (*Aporie*) of knowing *before* knowledge, with which Hegel reproached epistemology, now returns in Hegel's thought as an actual dilemma: namely, that phenomenology must in fact be valid prior to every possible mode of scientific knowledge.[28]

In effect, the Hegelian metacritical strategy is to construct a historically situated concept of legitimation rather than to presuppose one. However, the legitimacy of Hegelian phenomenology must, itself, be presupposed.

Hegel's defenders respond by pointing out that the *Science of Logic* begins with nothing other than pure indeterminacy, and that the conditions by which it legitimates itself, must be generated therefrom.[29] Nonetheless, Habermas' point seems to hold. The problem with the Hegelian strategy is that the speculative development of content from indeterminacy yields a vocabulary with an applicability to experience which must be presupposed. Even if we grant Hegel the claim that speculative content can be generated without reference to a determinate content, there is no guarantee that such content is legitimately used in speaking of our actual experience. On one side stands the edifice of Hegel's system; on the other stands the world. What is now needed is, precisely, some sort of Kantian deduction that would seek to question the legitimacy of applying the one to the other. Put differently, Hegel gives us no reason to think that the presuppositionless content of the *Science of Logic* bears any but homophonic resemblance to the content generated out of determinate experience in the *Phenomenology*.[30]

Moreover—and I will return to this point—it is not clear that, to situate the critique of reason, we must abandon Kant's transcendental project altogether. It remains to be seen whether and how a nonjuridical transcendental mode of inquiry might question the juridical model of critique. Even Kantian transcendental questioning is not as de-situated as his critics sometimes suggest. Hegel's judgment that, for Kant, critique is supposed to be presuppositionless may have been based too heavily on a Fichtean reading of the first *Critique*, for it is incorrect to characterize Kant's project as attempting to know before knowing. On the contrary, Kant begins precisely with the claim that we do, in fact, possess certain types of knowledge, concerning which he then, in effect, asks, "What can I know about knowing, given that I do know such-and-such?" Were this not so, Kant would not have consigned his bold affirmation of synthetic a priori knowledge to the introduction of the *Critique of Pure Reason*.

It is Heidegger who suggests a way of retrieving the type of situated transcendental inquiry which Kant undertook. In *Kant and the Problem of Metaphysics*, Heidegger goes so far as to make situatedness—under the guise of finitude—the central theme of Kantian inquiry. It is sometimes said that what distinguishes Heidegger from Kant is Heidegger's replacement of the Kantian subject with the view of Dasein as being-in-the-world. But, as Heidegger knows, this is Kant's startingpoint as well. What leads Kant from the standpoint of human finitude to his formulation of the idea of a disembodied transcendental subject is his reflection on what it means to be Dasein. Heidegger, of course, thinks that Kant failed to understand what it means to be Dasein because he failed to question the meaning of *Being* in the first place. The Kantian transcendental ego is a *result*—although one Heidegger takes exception to—of Kant's transcendental philosophy, not its startingpoint. In *Being and Time*, Heidegger seeks to undertake a mode of questioning that is still transcendental yet rooted in Dasein's being-in-the-world. It was this tension between the transcendental and the historically situated startingpoints of Heidegger that Husserl rejected. But it is just this idea— the idea of a historically situated transcendental inquiry— which suggests an alternative way of conceiving the Kantian project.

Where Kant assumes the legitimacy of a tribunal of reason, Heidegger attempts to radicalize the Kantian project by refusing to take any mode of questioning for granted. Of course, it is possible to read *Being and Time* as presupposing the legitimacy of the question of Being, but Heidegger cautions against presupposing that we know how to ask this question, and the entire book is nothing other than a sustained exercise in caution. The analytic of Dasein in the first division is merely provisional, and is, for that reason, criticized in the second division. Meanwhile, the second division develops a way of thinking about the Being of Dasein that is undermined in important ways by the end of the book. Of course, Heidegger never got to the third division of part one, so that, in the end, he never really formulates the question of Being. Read as a *Destruktion* of all ontology— including its own—*Being and Time* never legitimates anything.

Yet, at the same time, Heidegger never radicalizes the metadeductive question about how to think of juridical questions of legitimation. For instance, in his analysis of guilt he simply notes that this primordial state of Dasein's Being must not be grasped juridically. At crucial moments in his existential analytic, moreover, Heidegger ends up presupposing the same sort of juridical model as does Kant.

Reiner Schürmann illustrates this point. He reads Heidegger as seeking to articulate an *anarchic*—as opposed to a juridically *principled*—way of thinking and acting. Yet, as Schürmann shows, Heidegger ultimately remains committed to Kant's juridical model of *Deduktionsschriften*.

> For Kant, legitimation designates the procedure whereby *Rechtmässigkeit*, lawfulness, is assured in the usage of a priori concepts. This quest is the pivot on which his critical enterprise revolves. . . . Heidegger never repudiates the attempt to establish *legitimating categorial conditions* for "the very issue" of thinking.[31]

Heidegger's mode of questioning—as does Kant's—remains at the level of a juridically-based deduction rather than at the more radical level of a metadeduction:

> If the a priori so discovered is radically poorer than in any German philosophy prior to Heidegger, his way of laying it bare is still a deduction in the Kantian sense. . . . The legitimation of the anarchic origin requires a deduction.[32]

Even when Heidegger attempts to think beyond the juridical—when he tries to think anarchically—he falls back on a juridical model of legitimation.

Perhaps the political conservatism of both Hegel and Heidegger can be traced to their inability to radically question the juridical as such. Hegel's *Rechtsphilosophie* is rooted in juridical concepts which are never problematized. Despite the often convincing arguments by commentators who seek to show that Hegel's views were actually much more progressive that his writings suggest, his political philosophy begins from an inherited political ontology, the categories of which are drawn from the juridical systems of his day. If Hegel has his problems, Heidegger's political thought is also, on the most charitable interpretation, hopelessly deficient. That Heidegger failed to develop the resources for a radical political critique is so well known as to require little argument here. But perhaps we can suggest a link between Heidegger's political failures and his failure to raise the metadeductive question concerning the juridical.

None of what has been discussed here is meant to represent a dismissal of the unquestionably "redoubtable" work of Hegel and Heidegger.[33] Each develops a way of radicalizing the critical project that may very well prove to be fruitful for reworking the Kantian project once we have put it, so to speak, on proper metadeductive footing. However, neither Hegel nor Heidegger shows us how to raise the metadeductive question in an explicit way. Without asking this question it is difficult to see how we can fulfill the promise of the metacritical tradition—that is to genuinely radicalize critique. What remains unquestioned in the juridical model of Kant finds its parallel in something unquestioned in both Hegel and Heidegger.

Yet we still face the crucial problem which Habermas poses: how can a metadeductive inquiry avoid the performative contradiction of presupposing the very model it would challenge?

Chapter Two

From the Transcendental to the
Genealogical and Back:
Kant *avec* Foucault?

Is a radically nonjuridical questioning of the juridical model of critique even possible? After all, what would be the aim of such questioning? Would it not be to judge the legitimacy of critique's claim to be juridical? Yet such a task is, precisely, that of a juridical interrogation. To seek to judge the legitimacy of anything is to raise the *quid juris* question. Would a metadeduction simply posit a still higher court of appeal than that of the Kantian tribunal? For that matter, might the very act of judging itself be irreducibly juridical? If so, then a metadeductive questioning either must not seek to judge at all, or else it must thematize the possibility of a nonjuridical mode of judgment. However, is the latter really a genuine option? Could the former possibly tell us anything philosophically interesting?

Very schematically, there are three questions here that must be addressed. What is the relationship between: (1) judgment and the juridical; (2) critique and judgment; and (3) critique and the juridical?

Michel Foucault spent his entire career working through this very set of problems. In his archaeological phase, Foucault attempted to sever the connection between critique and judgment, producing texts that sidestep critique's traditional imperative to function juridically. Eventually, Foucault came to believe that the problem of the juridical and the problem of judgment were two separate issues. Judgment is misconceived when it is construed on a juridical model. Hence, with his genealogical turn, Foucault continued to develop a nonjudgmental critique, but he takes on the additional burden of articulating a nonjuridical theory of judgment—a theory with implications for a nonjuridical model of critique which he never fully formulated.

Throughout his career, Foucault associates the act of judging with the control of bodies, and he seeks to explicate the various ways in which discourses are used toward this end. This is already clear in *Madness and Civilization*, in which he tries to understand the ways in which a discourse of "madness" came into existence as a mechanism for the judging—and hence the subjugating—of bodies. In *Discipline and Punish*, he explains how an entire array of disciplinary mechanisms developed as ways of judging bodies. The famous figure of the panopticon serves as the image of a power that operates by an observation with a rule that is a type of judgment. Disciplinary power controls bodies by observing and classifying them, thereby reducing individual bodies to cases that can be uniquely manipulated.[1] The mechanism of such control is a normalizing judgment that assigns individual bodies their proper places in a classificatory grid. Thus, Foucault's famous "power/knowledge" equation is perhaps better described as a "power/judgment" equivalence, because judgment is the concrete effect of any discourse that counts as knowledge.

Where *Discipline and Punish* highlights the ways in which bodies are judged by techniques of observation, the first volume of *The History of Sexuality* focuses on ways in which bodies are trained to judge themselves. The imperatives to speak and to confess—both variants of Nietzsche's will to truth—are effects of a power that produces its effects through an imperative to self-judgment.

What is new in Foucault's genealogical texts is not the view that power is exercised through judgments. This view can be traced to his earliest writings. What is new, rather, is the thesis that the various forms of disciplinary power operate outside of traditional juridical institutions.

> Disciplinary power is opposed, . . . term by term, to
> a judicial penalty whose essential function is to refer,
> not to a set of observable phenomena, but to a corpus

of laws and texts that must be remembered; that operates not by differentiating individuals, but by specifying acts according to a number of general categories.[2]

Foucault is, thus, led to sever the traditional connection between power and the juridical precisely because he is led to discard the juridical model of judgment. Disciplinary judgments are not juridical laws or sentences, for their primary aim is not to repress. "The art of punishing, in the regime of disciplinary power, is aimed neither at expiation, nor even precisely at repression."[3] Rather, disciplinary judgments are productive. Instead of repressing, they exercise a control over bodies.

In the first volume of *The History of Sexuality* Foucault asks:

Why is this juridical notion of power, involving as it does the neglect of everything that makes for its productive effectiveness, its strategic resourcefulness, its positivity, so readily accepted? In a society such as ours, where the devices of power are so numerous, its rituals so visible, and its instruments ultimately so reliable, in this society that has been more imaginative, probably, than any other in creating devious and supple mechanisms of power, what explains this tendency not to recognize the latter except in the negative and emaciated form of prohibition? Why are the deployments of power reduced simply to the procedure of the law of interdiction?[4]

He answers these questions with the suggestion that "power is tolerable only on condition that it mask a substantial part of itself."[5] The juridical model simply masks the true functioning of disciplinary power.

Foucault thus rejects the juridical model of *power*, not because it links power with judgment, but rather because of the way in which it interprets the link between the two. Judgments do not have power because they invoke a law; judgments are themselves exercises of power. Foucault locates the source of this power, not in judicial institutions, but in disciplinary mechanisms. For instance, he finds the power to incarcerate not primarily in the courts, nor in the prisons themselves, but in all of the extrajuridical disciplines that emerged as ways of judging bodies. To understand the modern penal system, Foucault suggests, we would do better to focus on the various discourses of delinquency—medical, psychoanalytic, sociological, and the like—than on juridical institutions proper.

In *The Archaeology of Knowledge*, Foucault seems to have thought that a nonjuridical model of *critique* could be developed only by dispensing with the very category of judgment. Accordingly, he codifies archaeology as a way of questioning that is based on a methodological refusal either to study judgments or to produce judgments. Thus, on the one hand, the objects which archaeology purports to study are neither judgments nor sequences of judgments, but statements and discourses.

> The statement is not the same kind of unit as the sentence, the proposition, or the speech act; it cannot be referred therefore to the same criteria; but neither is it the same kind of unit as a material object, with its limits and independence. . . . It is not in itself a unit, but a function that cuts across a domain of structures and possible unities, and which reveals them, with concrete contents, in time and space.[6]

Just as archaeology takes statements rather than judgments to be its proper objects of study, so it refuses to render judgments about statements. The burden of an archaeology is not to judge but to distinguish, arrange, classify, and organize.

Unlike transcendental philosophy, which seeks the conditions for the possibility of judgments, archaeology will ignore judgments altogether and, instead, seek the conditions for the reality of statements. The search for transcendental conditions is the search for what Foucault calls a *formal a priori*. Diametrically opposed, archaeology seeks a set of conditions which Foucault labels the *historical a priori*.

> Juxtaposed these two words produce a rather
> startling effect; what I mean by the term is an *a
> priori* that is not a condition of validity for judgments,
> but a condition of reality for statements.[7]

For Foucault, this difference is crucial.

> In all of my work I strive . . . to avoid any reference
> to this transcendental as a condition for the possibility
> for any knowledge. . . . I try to historicize to the
> utmost in order to leave as little space as possible
> to the transcendental.[8]

While not ruling out the possibility of an eventual recourse
to the transcendental—"I cannot exclude the possibility that
one day I will have to confront an irreducible *residuum* which
will be, in fact, the transcendental"[9]—Foucault establishes,
as a cardinal methodological principle of archaeology, the
thesis that the transcendental move is to be deferred
indefinitely.

Because he viewed the positing of transcendental limits
as the heart of a juridical approach to critique, Foucault
repeatedly constrasted his own model of questioning with
that of Kant. In his essay "What is Enlightenment?,"
Foucault highlights these differences in detail. Enlightenment, he interprets Kant as saying, can be characterized
as an attempt to think beyond the limits of the present.
"Kant defines *Aufklärung* in an almost entirely negative way,
as an *Ausgang*, an 'exit,' a 'way out.'"[10] Agreeing with Kant
that philosophy should involve a thinking of limits, he
nonetheless insists on a mode of criticism that will owe
nothing to the transcendental.

> This criticism is not transcendental, and its goal is
> not that of making a metaphysics possible: it is
> genealogical in its design and archaeological in its
> method. Archaeological—and not transcendental—in
> the sense that it will not seek to identify the universal
> structures of all knowledge or of all possible moral
> action, but will seek to treat the instances of discourse
> that articulate what we think, say, and do as so many
> historical events. And this critique will be genealog-

ical in the sense that it will not deduce from the form of what we are what it is impossible for us to do and to know; but it will separate out, from the contingency that has made us what we are, the possibility of no longer being, doing, or thinking what we are, do, or think. It is not seeking to make possible a metaphysics that has finally become a science; it is seeking to give new impetus, as far and wide as possible, to the undefined work of freedom.[11]

In this rich passage, Foucault clarifies why he thinks of archaeology and transcendental philosophy as diametrically opposed. Transcendental philosophy is characterized as attempting to yield some sort of final judgment on what is possible and what is not. It construes limits as absolute and therefore unyielding rules as opposed to historical and contingent parameters. (Here I follow John McCumber's use of "parameter" as a "changeable or surpassable limit."[12]) As a matter of practical strategy, Foucault insists that we should call a limit to be historical until it is proven otherwise. In doing so, we give to the struggle to get out of the present a wider scope than if we were to fix present limits as irreducible features of the human condition.

In refusing to be either for or against the Enlightenment, Foucault wrestles with the question of whether a recast Kantian notion of Enlightenment could be interpreted as a type of strategy for resisting the determining forces of the present.

As an enterprise for linking the progress of truth and the history of liberty in a bond of direct relation, the Enlightenment formulated a philosophical question that remains for us to consider. . . . But that does not mean that one has to be "for" or "against" the Enlightenment. It even means precisely that one has to refuse everything that might present itself in the form of a simplistic and authoritarian alternative: you either accept the Enlightenment and remain within the tradition of its rationalism . . . or else you criticize the Enlightenment and then try to escape from its principles of rationality.[13]

Praising Kant's characterization of the problem of Enlightenment, Foucault interprets his "*Aude sapere*" as the challenge to determine "how the use of reason can take the public form it requires, how the audacity to know can be exercised in broad daylight, while individuals are obeying as scrupulously as possible."[14] But Foucault insists that his own method of critical inquiry serves as a better realization of the idea of Enlightenment than does Kant's. "The point, in brief, is to transform the critique conducted in the form of necessary limitation into a practical critique that takes the form of a possible transgression."[15] This means that Kant's transcendental mode of inquiry into the conditions for the possibility of experience must be transformed into an archaeological and genealogical inquiry into the historically determined conditions of our present experience.

> Archaeological—and not transcendental—in the sense that it will not seek to identify the universal structures of all knowledge or of all possible moral action, but will seek to treat the instances of discourse that articulate what we think, say, and do as so many historical events. And this critique will be genealogical in the sense that it will not deduce from the form of what we are what it is impossible for us to do and to know; but it will separate out, from the contingency that has made us what we are, the possibility of no longer being, doing, or thinking what we are, do, or think.[16]

The goal of such a critique, as we see again, is to promote the broadest notion of freedom.[17] The methodological refusal of the transcendental, thus, turns out to be an ethical principle, based on a practical postulate which affirms the desirability of struggle against limits. The regulative ideal of this principle would be a maximization of the potential for human freedom.

But this, of course, is precisely the same goal which drove Kant to develop his critical philosophy as transcendental. Underlying Foucault's explicitly antitranscendental philosophy, it would seem, is an ideal of human emancipation identical to Kant's. For Foucault, of course, this ideal cannot be presupposed as a transcendental limit on our thinking. However, if it is not transcendental, then Foucauldian method should require us to treat it as a prejudice of the present—that is, as something which we must think beyond. Obviously, there is a tension here in the fact that Foucauldian method is legitimated by an ideal which the method requires us to question. We face here the performative paradox of allowing a present limit to ground our obligation to question all limits. Would we not expect Foucauldian Enlightenment to challenge all practical ideals? Put differently, because Foucault does posit some ideal of freedom, why not call it "transcendental"?

Various versions of this problem have been voiced by those who express puzzlement about from where any basis for Foucault's implied practical ethic could come. Nancy Fraser asks, "Is [Foucault's] critique radically antifoundationalist, and if so, to what sort of justification can it lay claim?"[18] The fact that Foucault did not intend to advocate a general normative theory is evidenced in his advocacy of micropolitics and in the idea of the "specific intellectual," an ideal which he opposed to that of the "total intellectual," represented by the figure of Sartre.[19] As Fraser points out, however, Foucault cannot avoid presupposing some sort of general ethical claim about the worthwhileness of resisting power in the first place—whether on a grand scale or at the micro-level.

> Foucault calls in no uncertain terms for resistance to domination. But why? Why is struggle preferable to submission? Why ought domination to be resisted? Only with the introduction of normative notions of some kind could Foucault begin to answer such questions.[20]

Fraser goes on to note that Foucault sometimes seems to tacitly presuppose a Kantian normative theory, although one which is incompatible with Foucault's antifoundationalism.

> If one asks what exactly is wrong with [the disciplinary] society, Kantian notions leap imme-

diately to mind. When confronted with the treatment of persons solely as means that are causally manipulated by various institutions, one cannot help but appeal to such concepts as the violation of dignity and autonomy. But again, these Kantian notions are clearly related to the liberal norms of legitimacy and illegitimacy defined in terms of limits and rights.[21]

Agreeing with Fraser's assessment, Habermas suggests that even Foucault's descriptive claims cannot avoid an appeal to the transcendental.

In his basic concept of power, Foucault has forced together the idealist idea of transcendental synthesis with the presuppositions of an empiricist ontology. This approach cannot lead to a way out of the philosophy of the subject, because the concept of power that is supposed to provide a common denominator for the contrary semantic components has been taken from the repertoire of the philosophy of the subject itself. . . . Foucault cannot do away with all the aporias he attributes to the philosophy of the subject by means of a concept of power borrowed from the philosophy of the subject itself.[22]

On Habermas' reading, Foucault borrows both his theoretical notion of power and his practical notion of ethics from language games, the authority of which he simultaneously undermines.[23]

One way of presenting Foucault's problem is to say that he never quite manages to rise from something like a genealogy of pure reason to a genealogy of practical reason. As soon as he turns from descriptive claims to prescriptive claims, he keeps bumping up against transcendental issues which he would rather do without. Whether he meant to articulate an ethic at all was an issue about which Foucault felt uncertain, and, without a doubt, for just this reason. Yet, as his critics suggest, it is not clear whether his analyses can avoid the transcendental anyway.

The expressed reason for Foucault's antipathy to the transcendental, as we have seen, was his association of the transcendental with absolute limits. Because Foucault equates the juridical with a positing of fixed limits, we can also say that he associates the transcendental with the juridical. However, because he eventually comes to reject a juridical model of judgment, why not also challenge the juridical model of the transcendental? Perhaps Foucauldian Enlightenment can provide the means for an ethical position that would be both genealogical and transcendental?

What seems to prevent Foucault from making this move is his attitude to the power/judgment equation which remains even after we reject the juridical model of judgment. At times, Foucault seems to take the possibility of nonjuridical judging to be a sufficient basis for an ethical philosophy. At other times, he rather romantically seeks to refuse to make any judgments whatsoever, especially ethical ones. However, such romanticism amounts to little more than the dream of being outside of power altogether—and Foucault, himself, has done more than anyone else to disillusion us of this dream. The power/knowledge equation proves that even genealogy must, of itself, be an exercise of power—and, thus, an exercise of judgment. Hence, in the end, ethics may be just as ineluctable as power. It was when Foucault came to realize this, I think, that he hesitatingly undertook to articulate his care of the self-ethic, a topic to which I will return.

Gillian Rose sees Foucault's suspicions of the juridical as disingenuous because she sees him (and other poststructuralists) as merely trying to create some sort of "new legality" of their own—a burden which she sees as bequeathed to them by Nietzsche.

> Zarathustra's New Law Tables are called upon at critical moments in the work of Deleuze, Derrida and Foucault, who believe themselves to have accepted Nietzsche's challenge to renounce the ambition of previous philosophical labour to overcome the past, and instead to command and legislate the future.[24]

At times, Rose reads Foucault as wanting to establish his own laws. At other times, she reads him as nihilistically seeking to destroy all law. "Foucault is opposed to merely turning the table which opens up the space of the court-room—on the judge. He recommends that we smash it, and he is sanguine that the end of law, the *finis*, can be executed."[25] She supports this double reading by suggesting that every nihilistic attack on law inadvertently invokes a new law. "Like all nihilist programmes, this one insinuates a new law disguised as beyond politics." In the case of Foucault, Rose suggests, this new law is simply the rule of *power*, a term which, on Rose's reading, names "a force before justification or value." Because he refuses the critical resources of the Kantian tribunal, Foucault also ends up adhering blindly to legalistic models which he cannot question, such as the terminology of civil law.[26] In the end, "the nihilism which most explicitly engages with law would most dangerously blind us to it."[27]

Although I think Rose is right to question Foucault's absolute refusal of the transcendenal, her view of Foucault's concern with the juridical seems misplaced. Foucault's rejection of the juridical is not based on a desire to "smash" the law, nor is his ethic of "getting out of the present" best understood as an imperative to "get outside the law." Foucault rejects the juridical framework for understanding power because he believes that power is not essentially juridical. He then rejects the juridical model of critique because he sees its political questions as misplaced questions concerning the legitimacy of power. If power is not juridical, then a juridical-style questioning of the juridical entitle-ments to power can only lead us down a blind alley—one which prevents us from understanding the actual mech-anisms whereby disciplines of domination exert their forces. This is not to say that juridical mechanisms of power— or juridical models of questioning—are irrelevant, nor are they to be dismissed out of hand. Juridical institutions play a real role in a network of disciplinary regimes, and, in certain specific situations, questions of right and legitimacy may well be appropriate. However, if we are to understand how the juridical functions as an instrument of power, then a juridical model of questioning will be ineffectual.

The system of right, the domain of the law, are permanent agents of these relations of domination, these polymorphous techniques of subjugation. Right should be viewed, I believe, not in terms of a legitimacy to be established, but in terms of the methods of subjugation that it instigates.

The problem for me is how to avoid this question, central to the theme of right, regarding sovereignty and the obedience of individual subjects in order that I may substitute the problem of domination and subjugation for that of sovereignty and obedience.[28]

That Foucault sought to think beyond the limits of the present attests to his desire to critique the juridical as such. But to critique the juridical is not to be automatically antijuridical and certainly not to be nihilistic. For similar reasons, I would question Rose's reading of Foucault's relationship to Nietzsche.[29]

Recently, a number of commentators have suggested that Foucault's imperative to transcend the limits of the present leaves us with a type of Nietzschean aesthetic rather than an ethical model for practical judgment.[30] A difficulty with this interpretation, however, is that the imperative to escape the limits of the present poses the same problem for any model of judgment. Because all judgments either posit or derive from limits, the grounding of a Foucauldian aesthetic would face the same problems as would a Foucauldian ethic.

Here, I would agree with Rose's caution that a Nietzschean position cannot escape the juridical. On the contrary, the will-to-power can only issue in a type of will-to-legislate. In this respect, Nietzsche was closer to Kant than was Foucault, for both Kant and Nietzsche construe freedom as autonomy— that is, as a type of self-legislation. Foucault differs from both by rejecting a juridical approach to the question of freedom. With his borrowed ideal of Enlightenment, Foucault is also closer to Kant than he is to Nietzsche.

However, without recourse to the transcendental moment, Foucault is unable to specify either a general theory of power or to provide a general ethic. While we cannot accept Kant's juridical model of transcendental philosophy as it stands—at minimum, we would need historically situated reworking of its terms and aims—it may be that we can only begin to think of a theory of how to escape the present by making a transcendental leap of some sort. It is usually assumed that Kantian ethics can be construed only as ahistorical law-giving—perhaps, however, a nonjuridical version of Kantian ethics can be transplanted onto Foucauldian soil.

Habermas suggests that Foucault is guilty of performative contradiction because he seems to appeal to transcendental elements that his genealogical position would preclude. However, suppose we ask a prior question. Can the genealogical and the transcendental be made compatible? It remains to be seen whether the notion of Enlightenment that Foucault cautiously borrows from Kant might bring with it a transcendental resource that he could exploit, without, thereby, ending up with an ahistorical—or naively juridical—model of questioning. In order to imagine what a nonjuridical approach to the transcendental might involve, we need, first, to explicate the relationship between the transcendental and the juridical in Kant. Expressed otherwise, we must undertake a metadeduction of the juridical model of Kantian critique, using Foucauldian genealogy as our method of approach.

Because Foucault's rejection of the juridical model of power is equally a rejection of the juridical model of judgment, his analysis suggests a set of questions for the reading of Kant. If the juridical model of power masks the way in which power actually functions, what does this suggest about the juridical model of critique? If the former masks the true functioning of power, might the latter mask the true functioning of critique? If so, what is the true functioning of critique? What is the relationship between power and critique? Are the juridical judgments issued by the Kantian court of reason instances of disciplinary power in some sense? Might a questioning of the relationship between the juridical and the disciplinary in Kant provide a way to undertake a metadeductive reading of the juridical model of critique?

Chapter Three

The Role of Discipline in Kant's Court of Reason

What is the relationship between Kant's juridical model of critique and the juridical model of power? My hypothesis is this: Kant subscribes to the juridical model of power and he fashions critique on a juridical model so that it might serve as an instrument for resisting domination. Hence, the political stakes of critique consist primarily in a battle of laws. At the same time, Kant recognizes the emergence of disciplinary power, which, however, he continues to construe on a juridical model. As the key to critical philosophy's struggle with disciplinary power, Kant invokes a new form of discipline. Thus, the juridical battle between power (heteronomy) and critique (autonomy) becomes a struggle between two sorts of discipline—a discipline of domination (heteronomy) versus a discipline of resistance (autonomy).

So disciplined was the daily routine of Kant's own life that it could serve as a fitting figure for the age in which, according to Foucault, disciplinary power emerges as a new form of domination.[1] Foucault writes. "For the disciplined man, as for the true believer, no detail is unimportant."[2] One of Kant's contemporaries suggested that there may never have lived a person who paid as much attention to his body as did Kant.[3] From the moment he woke up (at 4:55 a.m. every day) until the instant when he fell asleep at night, no detail of his daily routine was too insignificant to escape disciplinary control.[4] In order to maximize the number of his actions that would be governed by principles, Kant had to monitor such minutiae as the manner in which he put his feet down on the pavement while on his famously punctual walk.[5] Apparently, one of his aims in life was never to perspire.[6]

For Foucault, one of the important differences between discipline as a means of correction and earlier forms of punishment is that the latter are primarily negative in the sense that they involve repression and restraint. Torture is the model for predisciplinary control of bodies. By contrast, discipline does not merely train by restraining or injuring. Rather, it is positive in the sense that it actively produces certain types of bodies. For this reason, one of Foucault's methodological general rules is "Do not concentrate the study of the punitive mechanisms on their 'repressive' effects alone, on their 'punishment' aspects alone, but situate them in a whole series of their possible *positive* effects."[7]

In a striking passage in the preface to the second edition of the first *Critique*, Kant notes that critique—itself a form of correction—can play a positive as well as a negative result. He also explicitly compares the role of critique to the role of the police.

> To deny that the service which the Critique renders is *positive* in character, would thus be like saying that the police are of no positive benefit, inasmuch as their main business is merely to prevent the violence of which citizens stand in mutual fear, in order that each may pursue his vocation in peace and security.[8]

The sense in which the police play a positive role over and above the negative, repressive function of preventing crime captures well the double sense which Kant associates not only with critique but with his conception of the discipline of critique.

Kant does not explicitly characterize discipline as productive. He still defines it as a form of negative instruction."[9] Nonetheless, in every branch of his philosophy as well as in his life, we find discipline playing a central role as a method that is both negative and positive. It is a means for eradicating error that culminates in the production of positive results. As such, discipline (*Disziplin*) always functions in tandem with its complement, *culture* (*Kultur*). Discipline works to extirpate bad habits through training by constraint (*Zucht*),[10] while culture encourages good habits.

> Discipline is distinguished from *culture*, which is intended solely to give a certain kind of skill, and not to cancel any habitual mode of action already present. Toward the development of a talent, which has already in itself an impulse to manifest itself, discipline will therefore contribute in a negative, culture and doctrine [*Doktrin*] in a positive, fashion.[11]

Culture is not the opposite of a merely negative discipline but rather its positive completion. Kant always discusses discipline and culture together, because he sees them as complementary tools that work in tandem. Hence, the function of discipline is not merely repressive. It functions as a type of leveling of instinct which prepares the way for a positive molding of a new set of instincts.

In the first *Critique*, Kant notes that reason is capable of constructing a canon only if it is first capable of censuring its errors. For this, the task of a discipline (*Disziplin*) of reason is required. Under the heading *Transcendental Doctrine of Method*, "discipline" is defined as a form of negative judgment designed to extirpate the systematic errors that are engendered by reason itself. The discipline of pure reason must take the form of a critical self-examination on the part of reason.

> Particular errors can be got rid of by *censure*, and their causes by *criticism*. But where, as in the case of pure reason, we come upon a whole system of illusions and fallacies, intimately bound together and united under common principles, a quite special negative legislation seems to be required, erecting a system of precautions and self-examination under the title of a *discipline*.[12]

Foucault stresses the important role that the *examination* comes to play in the emerging disciplines of the period. He describes the examination as "a surveillance that makes it possible to qualify, to classify and to punish. It establishes over individuals a visibility through which one differentiates them and judges them."[13] Kant characterizes the discipline of reason in explicitly juridical terms. The aim of discipline in the first *Critique* is to ensure that reason does not violate its own laws. "We are demanding of reason nothing but the *rule* of conduct."[14] (Deleuze concludes that it was Kant's aim in the first *Critique* to found a "civil state" of reason.[15])

Discipline plays an essential role in Kant's theory of moral development as well. Under the rubric of "education," Kant includes the nurturing of small children, disciplinary training (*Zucht*), and culture (*Bildung*).[16] He argues that a will can be taught to act independently of the determinations of the faculty of desire only if it has first been disciplined to do so. Disciplinary training is akin to the type of external coercion which Aristotle sees as a necessary condition for the inculcation of morally correct habits. Higher moral education—or what we might call moral education proper—requires culture, the primary aim of which is to teach children to act in accordance with maxims.

> Moral culture must be based upon "maxims," not upon discipline; the one prevents evil habits, the other trains the mind to think. We must see, then, that the child should accustom himself to act in accordance with "maxims," and not from certain ever-changing springs of action. Through discipline we form certain habits, moreover, the force of which becomes lessened in the course of years. The child should learn to act according to "maxims," the reasonableness of which he is able to see for himself. One can easily see that there is some difficulty in carrying out this principle with young children, and that moral culture demands a great deal of insight on the part of parents and teachers.[17]

Moral discipline can train us to act morally, but moral culture is needed to teach us to act in accordance with principles. To learn moral culture is not just to learn the right principles, although it is that, too. It is to learn to act in accordance with principles, period. In the "Doctrine of the Methods of Ethics" section of *The Metaphysics of Morals*, he outlines a program of moral discipline under the rubric of "Ethical Ascetics." The aim of ethical ascetics is twofold. Just as the discipline of pure reason is an attempt to extirpate the theoretical errors to which reason is naturally prone, so the discipline of ethical ascetics seeks to extirpate the tendencies of our inclinations to lead us into moral error. This is its first aim. Its second aim is to produce certain positive results—chiefly to promote a cheerful heart. "The rules for practicing virtue (*exercitorum virtutis*) aim at a frame of mind that is both *valiant* and *cheerful* in fulfilling its duties (*animus strenuus et hilaris*)."[18]

Thus, the principle of ethical ascetics is not "no pain, no gain," although, to a certain extent, it has the ring of "you will suffer and you will like it." Kant acknowledges that virtue does require "sacrificing many of the joys of life, the loss of which can sometimes make one's mind gloomy and sullen." And the injunction to cultivate the ever-cheerful heart is just that—a moral injunction. We are morally obliged to be cheerful. "What is not done with pleasure but merely as compulsory service has no inner worth for one who attends to his duty in this way."[19] Thus, the pursuit of cheerfulness is not merely incidental to the cultivation of virtue. This is in keeping with Foucault's claim that a distinguishing feature of discipline is its ability to train by rewarding as well as by punishing.

> In discipline, punishment is only one element of a double system: gratification-punishment. And it is this system that operates in the process of training and correction.[20]

Foucault characterizes discipline as "an art of the human body."[21] Whether others practice this art on us, or we on ourselves, disciplinary power is primarily an external form of power originating outside the body on which it is exercised. To subject one's own body to disciplinary control would therefore be a kind of heteronomy. However, for Kant, to pursue the discipline of ethical ascetics is a way of acting autonomously.

Kant contrasts his ethical ascetics with what he calls "monkish ascetics." The latter preaches loathing of oneself and recommends self-torture and mortification of the flesh. Such a program, Kant argues, "is not directed to virtue but rather to fantastically purging oneself of sin by imposing punishments on oneself." While monkish ascetics advocates the torturing of bodies, ethical ascetics involves the training of bodies. In recommending the discipline of ethical ascetics—the training of bodies—over torture, Kant conforms to the pattern which Foucault describes as a contemporaneous shift in penal mechanisms whereby the practice of punishing the bodies of criminals, often through torture, was replaced by discipline as a new form of correction.[22] Kant describes the discipline of ethical gymnastics as a practice whereby we train our bodies to enjoy acting virtuously. "Hence the training (discipline) that a man practices on himself can become meritorious and exemplary only through the cheerfulness that accompanies it."[23]

There are obvious reasons to be suspicious of the Kantian idea that practicing an ethic of denial and obedience to law should be a condition for the possibility of freedom. The notion that to act contrary to all one's inclinations is the way to freedom is certainly a different model from traditional theories which define freedom precisely as the ability to act in accordance on one's desires. It is easy to see why many critics have viewed the categorical imperative as just an internalized superego, an interpretation which quickly reduces its supposedly autonomous origin to a socially inscribed command.

Deleuze characterizes the categorical imperative, not as a superego, but as something comparable—a blind law which we are commanded to obey not because it is good but simply because it commands us to do so. To illustrate his point, he contrasts the ways in which Kant and Plato conceive of the relationship between the concepts of "good" and "law." For Plato, a law is merely a representative of the Good. A law must be evaluated in terms of the good and not vice versa. Knowledge of the good, for Plato, would make the introduction of laws unnecessary.[24] However, for Kant, the situation is reversed. We call something good because it conforms to the law.[25] It would not make sense to ask whether the categorical imperative is a good law, because all determinations of the good must be derived from it. Its emptiness makes it a law whose content we can neither know nor evaluate.

> The law does not tell us *what* we must do, it merely tells us "you must!," leaving us to deduce from it the Good, that is, the object of this pure imperative. But it is the Good which derives from the law, and not vice versa. As in Kafka's *The Penal Colony*, it is a determination which is purely practical and not theoretical. . . . We know it only through its imprint on our heart and our flesh: we are guilty, necessarily guilty.[26]

The categorical imperative turns out to be a brute given that cannot be evaluated. Of course, because Kant considers the categorical imperative to be *the* moral law, he would say that it is good by definition. However, this amounts to little more than saying that we have no choice but to acknowledge its absolute authority over us.[27] (The writing on bodies in Kafka's *Penal Colony* serves as a fitting image of Foucauldian discipline as an "art of the human body.")

Deleuze suggests that the works of both the Marquis de Sade and Leopold von Sacher-Masoch can be viewed as reactions to this eminently modern, Kantian construal of a moral law before which we are necessarily guilty.[28] The connection between Kant and Sade is of especial importance and has been postulated by a number of commentators. In terms of their specific aims, it would be hard to imagine two modes of discipline more different from each other than theirs. Kant's was a discipline in pursuit of virtue, while Sade's discipline aspired to vice. However, if they differ in the content of their aims, they are identical with respect to their form—a ruthless and thorough-going attention to detail in their regimented attempts to manipulate bodies. Kant's denial of the desires of the body seems to parallel Sadean punishment. As Horkheimer and Adorno show, both

Sadean and Kantian discipline advocate a principled and systematic self-control. Just as Kant recommends the cultivation of apathy as part of the requisite self-discipline needed for moral training, so does Sade's Juliette who "preaches on the self-discipline of the criminal."[29] "In regard to self-control, her directions are at times related to Kant's as the special application to its basic proposition."[30] Moreover, a disciplined, regimented order is the common ideal of both the Kantian and Sadean programs.

> The architectonic structure of the Kantian system, like the gymnastic pyramids of Sade's orgies . . . reveals a [sic] organization of life as a whole which is deprived of any substantial goal. These arrangements amount not so much to pleasure as to its regimented pursuit.[31]

Horkheimer and Adorno criticize what they take to be the excessive formalism of Kant's moral philosophy. Because the categorical imperative is posited as a pure law, we must supply it with content. Although only a very specific type of content will satisfy the categorical imperative, its emptiness reflects—and to some extent ushers in—a crisis in morality which Kant himself failed to recognize. "Kant had so far cleansed the moral law within me of all heteronomous belief, that respect for Kant's assurances was a mere natural psychological fact."[32] Kant believed that he was defending morality against its critics when, in fact, he was preparing its demise. Sade's systematic refutation of morality only carries out to its logical conclusion the "intransigent critique of practical reason, in contradistinction to which Kant's critique itself seems a revocation of his own thought."[33]

Lacan draws a similar comparison in his essay, "Kant with Sade." Lacan's argument also begins from an analysis of the formalism of Kantian morality. Observing "the paradox that it should be at the moment when the subject is no longer faced with any object that he encounters a law,"[34] Lacan goes on to give a psychoanalytic reading of a certain eroticism which he detects in Kant's "expression of the regret that, in the experience of the moral law, no

intuition offers a phenomenal object."[35] It is this same
eroticism which Lacan claims to find at work in Sade. He
concludes that Sade's work completes Kant's great work
on moral philosophy.[36] As did Deleuze, Horkheimer, and
Adorno, Lacan also affiliates Kant with Sade at the point
where Kant construes freedom as a certain type of obedience
to a pure law.

Although Kant does formulate an ethic of obedience,
however, he also seems to provide the resources for
distinguishing between two sorts of obedience—what we
might contrast as critical versus dogmatic obedience. After
all, what it means to "obey" the categorical imperative is
to resist—rather than obey—any law which runs contrary
to our moral duty. We should, therefore, expect Kant to
advocate a refusal of blind obedience before the laws of
the state. Yet, in his political philosophy, he does not seem
to pursue this path.

In "What is Enlightenment?" Kant argues that the
subjects of an enlightened state must obey its decrees
provided that they are granted the freedom to disagree
publicly with them. So long as subjects have this limited
freedom, the argument suggests, they must be willing to
relinquish all else. "For enlightenment of this kind, all that
is needed is *freedom*," but freedom is defined in the narrow
sense of the freedom to dispute what the state bids us to
do. Kant writes approvingly of Frederick, "Only one ruler
in the world says: *Argue* as much as you like and about
whatever you like, *but obey!*"[37]

Two years after the death of Frederick the Great, the
new and decidedly less enlightened king, Frederick William
II, appointed a new Minister of Justice—Johann Christoph
Wöllner, who succeeded the man to whom Kant had
dedicated the first *Critique*. The notorious Wöllner was
enlisted to help "stamp out the Enlightenment."[38] Deciding
that Kant's *Religion within the Limits of Reason* epitomized
Enlightenment thought, Wöllner threatened Kant with
censorship.

Kant issued a public report on his confrontation with
Wöllner—but only after Wöllner had been replaced—in the

preface to "The Conflict of the Faculties" published in 1798. In this report, he begins by recalling his earlier position on public and private responsibilities, pledging obedience to "an enlightened government, which . . . permits this work to be published now."[39] In the letter to Wöllner which he now reprints, Kant reveals that he had promised Wöllner *"as Your Majesty's most loyal subject"* not to publish anything having to do with religion. Had Kant merely capitulated? Not in his own eyes—for in a footnote, Kant informs the reader of his secret cunning in using the phrase "as Your Majesty's most loyal subject."

> This expression . . . I chose carefully, so that I would not renounce my freedom to judge in this religious suit *forever*, but only during His Majesty's lifetime.[40]

In contrasting the type of obedience he now pledges to the new minister with the type he had earlier promised to Wöllner, Kant seems to claim a consistency in principle. Yet, from whence would come this consistency?

So long as one has the freedom to dispute in public, Kant maintains, any further state limitations on freedom are tolerable. However, what happens to the private obedience/public disputation distinction when what the state demands is censorship? How can Kant obey the decree privately while retaining the right to publicize his disagreement? Only a performative contradiction could result from the attempt to obey a decree that commands one to silence while retaining the right to speak. So what Kant does is to *defer* his right to dispute publicly until Wöllner dies, thereby somehow retaining his claim to that right.

The sharp separation between private obedience and public dispute has been attacked by critics who note that the principle would oblige individuals to comply with decrees that order them to violate the categorical imperative. Adolf Eichmann's infamous invocation of Kant frequently comes to the fore in this context.[41] But defenders of Kant have sought to put his response to Wöllner in a more heroic light. Frederick Beiser, postulating Kant's fear of a broader censorship of his "fellow *Aufklärer*," suggests that Kant adjusted his politics in order to prevent further restrictions on freedom of the press.[42] Beiser suggests that "Kant could be fearlessly outspoken in the face of authority, so there is no reason to question his integrity."[43]

The real question, however, is not whether Kant violated his moral principles through cowardice. At issue is the inadequacy of Kant's principle—his advocacy of uncritical private obedience. For the crucial test case for Kant's public/private distinction is what policy it recommends in the threat of censorship—resistance or obedience. It is precisely on this issue that the theory lacks its crucial resources, and so appears to be far less radical than its defenders have claimed.[44] The inadequacy of the public/private distinction is its failure to recognize the difference between justified obedience and unjustified obedience.

On the other hand, Kant would seem to advocate resistance to anything that would reduce rational subjects to manipulable commodities with a "price."

> For unless the dignity of virtue is exalted above everything else in actions, the concept of duty itself vanishes and dissolves into mere pragmatic precepts, since man's consciousness of his own nobility then disappears and he is for sale and can be bought for a price that the seductive inclinations offer him.[45]

We should therefore expect Kantian ethics to advocate a vigilant resistance against the commodification of subjects—and, by extension, to any disciplinary domination. Kant's insistence on the difference between ethical ascetics and monkish ascetics would also seem to point toward the possibility of a discipline of resistance over and against a discipline of domination. It is monkish ascetics, not ethical ascetics, that we should expect to succumb to uncritical political obedience. We would expect ethical ascetics to strengthen our ability to resist forces of domination, rather than issue in some sort of will-to-become-a-docile-body.

We can trace Kant's failure to develop these potential resources for a genuine discipline of resistance to his juridical model of what it means to act critically. For Kant, we have an obligation to obey the law, period. However, we should not jump to blame the formalism of the categorical imperative. After all, the categorical imperative itself seems to be undermined by Kant's inability to distinguish between critical obedience and blind obedience. What we must understand is how Kant is led away from the categorical imperative to a valorization of obedience to law—and this we must trace to his seemingly uncritical embrace of the juridical in general. We also need to consider what alternative construal of Kantian ethics might result from a categorical imperative that bids us to develop a critical discipline of resistance instead of a dogmatic subservience to forces of domination.

Kant's ethical ascetics is, in effect, a juridical version of what Foucault calls "care for the self." In an interview conducted shortly before his death, Foucault used the word that Kant uses—*ascetical*—to describe a distinction between two different sorts of disciplining bodies. Just as Kant had contrasted ethical ascetics with monkish ascetics, so Foucault seeks to distinguish between an ascetical practice whereby a body would care for itself, and a technique of the self whereby a body is trained to make itself docile. Of the former, he says.

> It is what one might call an ascetical practice, giving the word "ascetical" a very general meaning, that is to say, not in the sense of abnegation but that of an exercise of self upon self by which one tries to work out, to transform one's self and to attain a certain mode of being.[46]

Yet, Foucault cautions against construing the care for the self as a liberating practice, on the grounds that the concept of liberation is a dangerous one. Moreover, exactly what an effective care-of-the-self ethic might involve Foucault does not specify.

While he refuses to characterize a care-of-the-self ethic as an all-encompassing strategy for resistance, his conception comes close to the idea of a discipline of resistance. That a Foucauldian could advocate any sort of disciplinary program as a means of resistance might seem strange to those who take his ethics to be an imperative to resist power in all its forms. However, for Foucault, power is ubiquitous and not an a priori evil.[47] It is when power manifests itself as domination that Foucault recommends that we resist it. He thus speaks of the "duty" of philosophy as "the challenging of all phenomena of domination at whatever level or under whatever form they present themselves."[48]

In refusing to construe all power as evil, Foucault was probably thinking less of Kant than of Nietzsche. As did Kant, Nietzsche also contrasts a type of good ascetic ideal (the discipline of the artist) with a bad ascetic ideal (the discipline of the priest). Nietzsche's distinction maps nicely onto Kant's distinction between ethical ascetics and monkish ascetics, with the obvious difference being that, for Nietzsche, the ethical is associated with the priestly. However, from a Foucauldian perspective, the question would be whether Kant's or Nietzsche's distinction provides the more effective strategy for resisting domination. It would also seem that both Kant and Nietzsche have their strengths and weaknesses here. Certainly the ease with which the Nietzschean aestheticization of power could be appropriated for domination as well as resistance made Foucault more cautious about calling himself a Nietzschean than, did, say, Deleuze.

Up until a certain point, both Kant and Nietzsche have the same basic idea—to become free, one must first resist heteronomous forces. (Hence, in *Zarathustra*, the spirit must become a lion before it becomes a child.) This can be done by practicing one type of discipline against another. A certain way of actively caring for the self is to avoid being a merely reactive body. Both Kant and Nietzsche believed that they practiced the right type of discipline, and they sought to teach others by their own examples—Nietzsche in *Ecce Homo* and Kant in the third essay of "The Conflict of the Faculties." It is interesting that all three—Kant, Nietzsche, and Foucault—articulate the need to cultivate a certain care for the self in their last writings.[49]

In "The Philosophy Faculty versus the Faculty of Medicine," Kant tries to show how his own care of the self—his moral discipline—could serve as a way of producing a healthy body. He suggests how a "morally practical philosophy" can produce a "panacea" (*Universalmittel*) for avoiding physical ailments.[50]

> This panacea, however, is only a *regimen* (*Diätetik*) to be adopted: in other words, it functions only in a *negative* way, as the art of *preventing* disease. But an art of this sort presupposes, as its necessary condition, an ability that only philosophy, or the spirit of philosophy, can give.[51]

Despite his characterization of his regimen as negative, it is designed to produce a healthy body. The regimen is negative only in the sense that it does not cure an illness, but rather prevents the onset of disease. Thus, Kant's regimen is explicitly put forth as an experiment in what Foucault calls "bio-power." The rest of the essay consists of an argument for his own care of the self. Kant recommends his own manner of sleeping, walking, breathing—one apparently can learn to "drink air" by breathing through one's nostrils—eating, and so on.

> My examples . . . cannot be drawn from other peoples' experiences, but, in the first instance, only from what I have experienced in myself; for they come from introspection, and only afterwards can I ask others whether they have not noticed the same thing in themselves. I am forced, accordingly, to talk about myself; and although this would betray lack of modesty in a dogmatic treatise, it is excusable if we are dealing, not with common experience, but with an inner experiment or observation that I had to make on myself before I could submit, for others' consideration, something that would not of itself occur to everyone unless his attention were drawn to it.[52]

Here Kant anticipates the criticism that he is presenting the public with just another dogmatic primer on how to perform basic bodily functions. True to his view that the need to follow someone else's—even his own—nutritional guidelines is a mark of immaturity,[53] he reminds his readers that they must verify the usefulness of his recommendations for themselves.

Robin Schott suggests a Foucauldian reading of this text, one which sees Kant's recommendations as so many techniques of the self.

> Kant discusses in detail how to breathe through the nose rather than the mouth and how to swallow so as to preserve saliva. In Kant's view, one walks for the sake of proper digestion; one's every breath is taken with an eye to the consequences for one's head and throat. These stratagems serve the health and longevity of the body with which, as Foucault notes, the eighteenth-century bourgeoisie were inordinately concerned.[54]

By Schott's analysis, Kant's ascetic care of the self is the result of his repudiation of the sensuous and sensual. While her argument is compelling—and I agree with her conclusions—I would highlight the fact that Kant's various strategies are intended to function as ways of resisting disciplinary control of bodies. His overarching aim, after all, is to obviate the need for medical intervention in people's lives. Kant's text can cut two ways. On the one hand, it reads like just another primer for how to make oneself a docile body. At the same time however, it purports to be a guideline for how to keep one's body free from medical intervention. To be sure, teaching bodies to exercise bio-power on themselves is not to liberate them from bio-power. Kant is, however, attempting to articulate a bio-power of resistance, even if he ends up advocating a bio-power of domination. In this, he also anticipates Foucault's attempt to articulate a care-of-the-self ethic. What must be seen is how Kant's attempted discipline of resistance degenerates into a discipline of domination. To see this, we also must take a closer look at Kant's own life.

Chapter Four

The White Wall above Me and the Black Hole within Me: Kant's Care of the Self

In "What is Enlightenment?" Kant contrasts critical living with dogmatic living, suggesting that to allow "a doctor to judge my diet for me" would be a sign of "immaturity" in the sense of living uncritically.[1] Kant's care of the self—his practice of ethical ascetics—purports to be a way of living critically. However, the aim of his program is not, primarily, to free his body from the heteronomous influence of external forces of domination—such as, for example, the coercion of medical technologies. For Kant, the primary threat to freedom comes, precisely, from our own bodies.

To be autonomous, the will "must be conceived as wholly independent of . . . the law of causality. Such independence is called *freedom* in the strictest, i.e., transcendental, sense." To the extent that our bodies are subject to the laws of nature, they can only be heteronomous influences on the will. All of our desires, it turns out, are subject to the laws of nature in this way. They are always naturally constituted because "we cannot know, a priori, of the idea of any object . . . whether it will be associated with pleasure or displeasure or will be merely indifferent."[2] Nature, of course, has designed us in such a way that we are constantly motivated to act on our desires, but the natural goal of humanity is to cultivate a good will.[3] An effective care of the self must therefore defend the will from any incursion by its natural enemy—the desires of the body.[4]

Interestingly, Antonin Artaud puts forth a strikingly similar notion of freedom as does Kant. The idea of a "body

48

without organs" is invoked by Artaud to describe the sort of thing which he thinks a person must become in order to transcend the "automatic reactions" of his body. Artaud writes, "When you will have made him a body without organs,/then you will have delivered him from all his automatic reactions and restored him to his true freedom."[5]

Gilles Deleuze and Félix Guattari use Artaud's notion of a body without organs to articulate the dynamics of a certain logic of desire. We can use their vocabulary to plumb the depths of Kant's war against his body. For Deleuze and Guattari, a body without organs is something produced by desiring. As such, it is neither good nor bad. Once produced, it functions as a type of "surface" upon which a body can experience the "intensities" or "becomings" which issue from our desiring.[6] Becomings are "what happens on each type of body without organs, in other words, the modes, the intensities that are produced, the waves that pass."[7] Deleuze and Guattari also conclude that the kinds of becomings experienced will vary depending on the type of body—for example, the only kinds of becomings that a masochist body without organs can experience are pains. A "full" body without organs is capable of experiencing becomings of some sort. An "empty" one is incapable of doing so.

By striving to produce a body that will not allow itself to be influenced by its desires, Kant, in effect, aspires to the state of an empty body without organs. To be sure, Kant does not argue that we are morally obliged to eliminate our desires altogether. However, in order to prevent them from determining our will, we must steel ourselves against their effects. We must, therefore, not allow ourselves to enjoy the pleasurable intensities or becomings that might flow on our bodies.

To cultivate a good will is, precisely, to train one's body not to experience the effects of its desires. As does the masochist, Kant's daily routine is a program for replacing instinctive forces with transmitted forces.[8] Not only will he awaken precisely at 4:55 every morning, but he will not feel the slightest inclination to go back to sleep. Not only will he limit himself to one cup of tea, but he will not desire a second cup of tea. Yet unlike the masochist—who at least gets to experience pains as becomings—Kant forbids himself from experiencing any type of becomings. In this context, he invokes the example of the Stoics. "The principle of apathy, that is, that the prudent man at no time be in a state of emotion, not even in that of sympathy with the woes of his best friend, is an entirely correct and sublime moral precept of the Stoic school."[9]

The ideal of making himself an empty body is, of course, a mere limit that Kant can never fully achieve. It is an ideal in the exact sense in which acting from duty is an ideal. Try as he might, he cannot prevent himself from experiencing becomings altogether. The constant aim of Kant's care of the self, then, must consist in taming these unlawful becomings. This means submitting them to the rule of law.

To understand what this process involves, we must look more closely at what exactly a "becoming" is. Deleuze derives his usage of the term from the Stoics:

> The Stoics . . . distinguish between two kinds of things. First, there are bodies . . . and the corresponding "states of affairs." . . . *The only time of bodies and states of affairs is the present.* . . . Second, all bodies . . . are causes of certain things of an entirely different nature . . . not things or facts, but events. . . . They are not living presents, but infinitives: the unlimited Aion, *the becoming which divides itself infinitely in past and future and always eludes the present.* Thus time must be grasped twice, in two complementary though mutually exclusive fashions.[10]

Both Deleuze and Guattari use the Stoic concept of becomings to characterize the flows which subsist across time rather than exist in any fixed present moment.

In Kant, we find a slightly different distinction from the one drawn by the Stoics. Because time is the pure form of inner (but not outer) intuition, objects in space—that is, things as they appear to us—are only in time to the extent that our representations of them are in time.

Time is not something which exists of itself, or which inheres in things as an objective determination. . . . It cannot be a determination of outer appearances. . . . But since all representations, whether they have for their objects outer things or not, belong, in themselves, as determinations of the mind, to our inner state; and since this inner state stands under the formal condition of inner intuition, and so belongs to time, time is an *a priori* condition of all appearance whatsoever.[11]

Bodies (appearances in space) exist outside of time, but they are subject to time as a condition for our representing them to ourselves. Insofar as they are subject to time, bodies undergo becomings, but these becomings should, by right, subsist, not in the bodies themselves, but in the subject's experience of them. In this way, the becomings of the body would be ruled by the Kantian subject rather than the other way around.

Deleuze suggests that the phrase *The time is out of joint*, from *Hamlet*, aptly characterizes Kant's view of time.

Time is out of joint, time is unhinged. . . . As long as time remains on its hinges, it is subordinate to movement. . . . It is now movement which is subordinate to time. Everything changes, including movement. We move from one labyrinth to another."[12]

Everything changes. For Heraclitus, this means that everything is in a state of becoming. For Kant, however, it means the exact opposite. By making movement subordinate to the pure form of time, Kant would seek to reduce the becomings of bodies to the law-governed experience of a transcendental subject. Moreover, by thus regulating the flow of becomings, time itself would play a moral role in Kant's disciplinary regimen. As Deleuze observes, "The law as empty form in the *Critique of Practical Reason* corresponds to time as pure form in the *Critique of Pure Reason*."[13]

However, despite the regulating clock of the pure form of time, Kant finds that his body still experiences unlawful becomings. Desires produce effects which escape the moral/ temporal law. Here is where his care of the self must intervene. Its goal will be to extend the dominion of the law of time over these recalcitrant becomings. Kant adopts a training maxim: all events—all becomings—will be governed by the clock, by lawfully measured time.

> Precisely at five minutes before five o'clock, winter and summer, Lampe, Kant's footman, who had formerly served in the army, marched into his master's room with the air of a sentinel on duty, and cried aloud, in a military tone, "Mr. Professor, the time is come."[14]

According to Wasianski, Lampe would announce *"mit dem ernsten militärischen Zuruf: 'Es ist Zeit!'"*[15] It is time. Because duty requires that we reduce becomings to law-governed instants, the call of time functions as a veritable alternative formulation of the categorical imperative for Kant. Naturally, Kant must answer this call immediately.

> This summons Kant invariably obeyed without one moment's delay, as a soldier does the word of command—never, under any circumstances, allowing himself a respite, not even under the rare accident of having passed a sleepless night.[16]

To ensure against the unlikely event of weakness of will, Kant instructed his servant to assist him in his self-disciplining.

> His servant had strict orders never to let him sleep longer than five, however strongly he might plead for more rest. . . . With a degree of pride he would sometimes ask the servant, in the presence of his guests, whether in thirty years he had ever been obliged to wake him twice? His answer was, "No, very noble Professor!"[17]

Thus, the least significant detail of his life must be governed by the law of time.

> Everything had its appointed time; and the neighbours knew that it was exactly half-past three when

Kant, in his grey coat and with the Spanish reed
in his hand, stepped out of his door and walked
towards the small Linden Avenue. . . . Eight times
he walked up and down there, at all seasons of the
year; and when the weather was unfavourable or
the grey clouds portended rain, his old servant,
Lampe, might be seen wandering anxiously behind
him, with a long umbrella under his arm, like a picture
of Providence.[18]

Even his manner of walking must be attended to carefully.

In order to walk more firmly, he adopted a peculiar
method of stepping: he carried his foot to the ground,
not forward, and obliquely, but perpendicularly, and
with a kind of stamp, so as to secure a larger basis,
by setting down the entire sole at once.[19]

The event of stepping is being reduced to a series of
measured instants. The parts of his foot will be retrained
to step as one—not heel first, then the ball of his foot,
then the toes—but all at once as a unified, law-governed
stepping machine.[20]

Any failure to reduce becomings is a painful experience
for Kant.

Oftentimes melodies, which he had heard in earliest
youth sung in the streets of Königsberg, resounded
painfully in his ears, and dwelt upon them in a way
from which no efforts of abstraction could release
him.[21]

A melody is an object of intuition that unfolds over time.
It is impossible to reduce a melody to a mere succession
of tonal instants. We can only hear it as an essentially
temporal unfolding—as a becoming. The only music that
Kant could tolerate were military marching songs, for these
at least measured out a clear, lawful beat, as if nailing each
note to its present, static moment. However, silence
bothered him too, for the amorphous absence of sound is
experienced as a becoming and, therefore, as "an oppression." Kant tried to solve the problem by sleeping with "a

repeater in his room. The sound was at first too loud, but means were taken to muffle the hammer; after which both the ticking and the striking became companionable sounds to him."[22] The repeater measures time. It structures durations in accordance with law. Is it any wonder that Kant never once in his life dared to venture out of sight of the clock-tower of Königsberg?

However, Kant cannot completely reduce becomings to law-governed series of moments. As time flows on—as opposed to marches on—he begins to develop an intensely phobic panic against the temporal as such. To combat his becomings, Kant, in effect becomes a speed-freak. Everything must be sped up, for, to endure a duration as a duration has become intolerable. Waiting for coffee—a form of speed, we might note—seems to be particularly excruciating.

> Coffee must be brought "upon the spot" (a word he had constantly in his mouth during his latter days) "in a moment."[23] And the expressions of his impatience . . . had so much of infantine *naïveté* about them. . . . A trifling delay seemed unendurable to Kant. . . . If it was said, "Dear professor, the coffee will be brought up in a moment"—"*Will* be!" he would say, "but there's the rub, that it only *will* be: 'Man never *is*, but always *to be* blest.'" If another cried out, "The coffee is coming immediately," "Yes," he would retort, "and so is the next hour: and, by the way, it's about that length of time that I have waited for it." Then he would collect himself with a stoical air, and say, "Well, one can die after all: it is but dying; and in the next world, thank God! there is no drinking of coffee, and consequently no waiting for it."[24]

Kant cannot tolerate any event of coffee-becoming. "*Auch das Kaltwerden des Kaffees*"—even the becoming-cold of coffee—seems to take too much time.[25] His relationship to coffee is like that of Alice's to jam. "The present always being eluded—'jam tomorrow and jam yesterday'—but never jam *today*."[26] When the time for coffee-drinking finally comes, Kant must gulp it down at once. "*Und hiermit Basta! welchen*

Ausdruck er mit einem Tempo, mit er die Tasse stark hinsetzte, gewöhnlich begleitete."[27]

One day Kant gets into a carriage with Wasianski.

The order of the day with Kant was, "Distance, distance. Only let us go far enough," said he: but scarcely had we reached the city-gates, before the journey seemed already to have lasted too long. On reaching the cottage, we found coffee waiting for us; but he would scarcely allow himself time for drinking it, before he ordered the carriage to the door; and the journey back seemed insupportably long to him, though it was performed in something less than twenty minutes. "Is this never to have an end?" was his continual exclamation.[28]

Mention is made of his coming birthday. Kant refuses to wait. He insists that they celebrate his birthday immediately. The party must take place "'upon the spot;' and he is not satisfied till the party was actually assembled."[29]

The only time when Kant seems to allow himself to experience a kind of becoming is at night, when he prepares himself for sleep. De Quincy describes the process as follows:

A quarter of an hour before retiring for the night, he withdrew his mind as much as possible from every class of thoughts which demanded any exertion or energy of attention. . . . He undressed himself without his servant's assistance. . . . This done, he lay down on a mattress, and wrapped himself up in a quilt. . . . Long practice had taught him a very dexterous mode of *nesting* and enswathing himself in the bedclothes. First of all, he sat down on the bedside; then with an agile motion he vaulted obliquely into his lair; next he drew one corner of the bedclothes under his left shoulder, and, passing it below his back brought it round so as to rest under his right shoulder; fourthly, by a particular *tour d'adresse*, he operated on the other corner in the same way; and finally contrived to roll it round his whole

person. Thus swathed like a mummy, or (as I used
to tell him) self-involved like a silk-worm in its
cocoon, he awaited the approach of sleep, which
generally came on immediately.[30]

What we might describe as the becoming-silk-worm of Kant
begins when he ceases to think—when the court of reason
closes down for the night. Kant's human faculties—his
"transcendental organs," as it were—are shut down as his
body sprouts the faculty of cocoon-spinning. On De
Quincey's reading, the becoming-silk-worm is mixed with
other animal-becomings. He refers to Kant's "nesting" and
speaks of his bed as a "lair."[31] Once the cocoon is spun,
a peaceful sleep comes on almost immediately. "No uneasy
passion ever arose to excite him, nor care to harass, nor
pain to awake him."[32] One of the aims of this program of
noctural bondage, apparently, was to prevent Kant from
accidentally masturbating in his sleep. However, before
nodding off, Kant surveys his handiwork, and, in De
Quincey's felicitous paraphrasing of Wasianski, he "ejacu-
lates" with pleasure about how wonderfully healthy he is.

> Kant's health was exquisite; not mere negative
> health, or the absence of pain . . . but a state of
> positive pleasurable sensation, and a conscious
> possession of all his vital activities. Accordingly, when
> packed up for the night in the way I have described,
> he would often ejaculate to himself (as he used to
> tell us at dinner)—"Is it possible to conceive a human
> being with more perfect health than myself?"[33]

It is only when he nears sleep that Kant feels the surge
of *jouissance* which manifests itself in the "ejaculation" about
how healthy he is. Indeed, it would almost seem as if Kant's
entire daily regimen body were designed for this momentary
ejaculation of pleasure, followed by a good critical slumber.
(As such, his care of the self would be like that of the sage
who preaches the virtue of sleep in Nietzsche's *Zarathustra*.[34])
Kant is moved to admire his health at the very moment
when his body has been freed from its juridical faculties.
However, the court of reason can go to sleep only after

having locked Kant's undisciplined body up for the night.[35] This, after all, will be a critical slumber—as opposed to the type of "dogmatic slumber" from which Kant claims to have awakened.[36]

Deleuze reminds us of Nietzsche's characterization of Kantian critique. "It is a 'justice of the peace's' critique" because it seeks to defend the idea of law at all costs. "The only object of Kant's critique is justification, it begins by believing in what it criticizes."[37] The fact that Kant seems to find satisfaction only in obeying the law lends support to a Lacanian reading. In his essay, "Kant with Sade," Lacan recounts how, in the *Critique of Practical Reason*, Kant bases morality on a renunciation of the faculty of desire. The categorical imperative cannot be satisfied by a maxim legislating the universal pursuit of pleasure. "No phenomenon can claim for itself a constant relation to pleasure. Thus, no law of such a good can be enunciated which would define as will the subject who would introduce it into his practice."[38] To this extent, there is a certain prohibition against the pursuit of pleasure in Kant. However, as we saw in the last chapter, Kant explicitly argues against the sort of monkish ascetics which would forbid us from pursuing pleasure altogether. In fact, the moral law requires that we strive to be happy. Taking stock of this simultaneous prohibition against desire and invocation to invest desire in obeying this prohibition, Lacan sees in Kant "a specification of the moral law which, looked at more closely, is simply desire in its pure state, that very desire that culminates in the sacrifice, strictly speaking, of everything that is the object of love in one's human tenderness."[39]

According to Kant, we cannot universalize a maxim that would bid us to pursue the objects of our desires because we cannot imagine a world in which everyone achieves the objects of their desires. On Lacan's reading, the categorical imperative commands the subject to renounce the pleasure principle and enter the Symbolic realm. This law bars us from the *jouissance* of transgression, while at the same time commanding us to find *jouissance* in our submission to the

Law of the Father. For Kant, this would be the substitution of a "higher" desire for a "lower" one.

Slavoj Žižek comments, "This Kantian moral imperative conceals an obscene superego injunction: 'Enjoy!'—the voice of the Other impelling us to follow our duty for the sake of duty is a traumatic irruption of an appeal to impossible *jouissance.*"[40] Žižek continues:

> . . . what remains hidden in Kant is the way this renunciation itself produces a certain surplus-enjoyment (the Lacanian *plus-de-jouir*). Let us take the case of Fascism—the Fascist ideology is based upon a purely formal imperative: Obey, because you must! In other words, renounce enjoyment, sacrifice yourself . . . you must find positive fulfillment in the sacrifice itself. . . . It is this renunciation, this giving up of enjoyment itself, which produces a certain surplus-enjoyment.[41]

When Kant says that we cannot universalize a maxim that would bid us to act from desire, he is pointing out that there are incompatible desires. However, he does not rule out the possibility of a world in which everyone's desires could be compatible. On the contrary, it is our duty to promote the *summum bonum*, and this means envisioning a world in which everyone would be happy. We are morally obliged to act as if we were constructing a world in which everyone's desires could be satisfied. Such a world might turn out to be merely imaginary—in either a Kantian or Lacanian sense—but its possible realization must be presupposed, not precluded.

As such, the kingdom of ends is less a Symbolic representation of a law-governed society than it is a kind of Imaginary realm in which external law becomes irrelevant. However, one could attribute this irrelevance to the fact that the kingdom of ends is the representation of a world in which everyone has already been completely Oedipalized. For in it, we are entitled to experience only such *jouissance* as does not involve our transgressing the Law. We can wish happiness only for those—including ourselves—whose desires are "worthy."[42] One recognizes the

Law of the Father not as the logical impossibility of a world in which everyone's desires would be satisfied, but as the prohibition against acting in accordance with those of our desires that would transgress the law. So long as everyone invests their desires in obeying the law, we can posit the possibility of universal *jouissance*.

Although a Lacanian reading can thus explain how it is that Kant takes pleasure in obeying the law, it has nothing to say about where Kant goes wrong. Instead of helping to diagnose the case of Kant, the Lacanian model merely uses this case to buttress its own theory of desire. For Kant's total renunciation of desire would simply represent an extreme expression of a successful process of Oedipalization.

Against Lacan, Deleuze and Guattari argue that successful Oedipalization is merely a way of subjugating bodies. They view Lacanian psychoanalysis as politically reactionary because it helps subjects become Oedipalized—that is, it trains bodies to think of their desires as infantile wishes rather than as ways of being that can challenge social and political forces of domination. To become Oedipalized is simply a way of succumbing to a discipline of domination, which functions in terms of a depoliticization of desire. Deleuze and Guattari accordingly oppose Lacan's depoliticized notion of desire as ineffectual lack with a notion of desire as productive and liberating.[43]

Deleuze and Guattari also notice something different about Kant's conception of desire compared with that of Lacan. "Kant . . . must be credited with effecting a critical revolution as regards the theory of desire, by attributing to it 'the faculty of being, through its representations, the cause of the reality of the objects of these representations.'"[44] Against Lacan and the "Platonic logic of desire," Kant conceives of desire, not in terms of acquisition—which implies need and therefore lack—but in terms of production. However, Kant fails to credit desire with the power to produce any real effects. Desire can only produce imaginary effects:

> It is not by chance that Kant chooses superstitious beliefs, hallucinations, and fantasies as illustrations

of this definition of desire: as Kant would have it, we are well aware that the real object can be produced only by an external causality and external mechanisms. . . . Hence it can be said that Kant's critical revolution changes nothing essential: this way of conceiving of productivity does not question the validity of the classical conception of desire as a lack.[45]

Despite Kant's failure to conceive of desire as capable of producing real effects, we can, however, see in his positing of desire's having imaginary effects the potential basis for a reworking of the criteria for realizing universal *jouissance*. An Imaginary vision that would begin otherwise than from the Lacanian Law of the Father.

In positing the kingdom of ends as a realm in which everyone's desires would be compatible with everyone else's, Kant affirms precisely what Lacan denies—the possible realization of universal *jouissance*. However, he can only posit this world as if it were populated by empty bodies, whose only pleasure comes in their respect for the law.

Thus, in the end, Kant ends up where Lacan finds him. But how did he get there? In attempting to understand the disciplinary mechanisms that lead to the construction of empty bodies, Deleuze and Guattari call attention to what they call the "three great strata . . . that most directly bind us: the organism, signifiance, and subjectification. . . . You will be organized, you will be an organism. . . . You will be signifier and signified. . . . You will be a subject, nailed down as one."[46] These three strata are what we might call the primary effects of a discipline of domination.[47] Disciplinary power exercises its dominion over bodies by organizing them, by giving them a certain significance or meaning, and by requiring them to function as isolated individual subjects. A full body is one that manages to escape these effects.

Kant, we might say, remains bound by the strata of signifiance and subjectification. The law-giving court of reason serves, in effect, as the instrument whereby Kant's body is colonized by forces that turn him into a docile citizen. His faculties, equipped with a predetermined set of categories and ideas, function as forces of signifiance. The strata of subjectification are those forces that turn Kant's situated body into a merely transcendental subject. Kant's body disappears into the singularity of the transcendental unity of apperception, subject to the law of organized time.

"The strata constitute the Judgment of God," Deleuze and Guattari write, alluding to the title of Artaud's "To have done with the judgment of God."[48] To truly have done with "the judgment of God"—or, we might say, to escape forces of domination—would require a destratification of the body. To some extent, Kant's care of the self seeks just this, but his discipline of resistance turns into a discipline of domination as his destratifications turn into restratifications. "Every undertaking of destratification (for example, going beyond the organism, plunging into a becoming) must therefore observe concrete rules of extreme caution: a too-sudden destratification may be suicidal, or turn cancerous."[49] The schizophrenic destratifies too quickly, and so plunges into what Deleuze and Guattari call a "black hole."[50] "The black hole is what captures you and does not let you get out."[51]

The corollary of a black hole is a "white wall." A white wall is a blank surface that cannot be read or crossed. The black hole is, in effect, a condition for the possibility of subjectification, and the white wall is a condition for the possibility of signifiance.

> Signifiance is never without a white wall upon which it inscribes its signs and redundancies. Subjectification is never without a black hole in which it lodges its consciousness, passion, and redundancies. Since all semiotics are mixed and strata come at least in twos, it should come as no surprise that a very special mechanism is situated at their intersection. Oddly enough, it is a face: the *white wall/black hole* system.[52]

We could imagine just such a system constructed by Kant's court of reason. The white wall would be the screen that separates phenomena from noumena, the limiting forms of intuition upon which experience gets written. Experience would be the site of signifiance, a function

automatically performed by the categories of the understanding. Specific meanings would be spontaneously forced
upon a subject who can neither invent new categories nor
get beyond the blank screen of space and time. At the same
time, Kant's self would be trapped in the singular unity
of transcendental apperception, and reduced to an empty
point, the black hole of the "I think." Its exit points would
be closed off at both ends. Neither the empirical ego nor
the idea of the subject as a thing in itself (a soul) could
give it a true line of flight. Kant's inability to think of his
situated body as the true subject of critique might be what
gets him into this trap in the first place.

Watching over—and listening to—the subject would be
the law, which manifests itself as the prohibition against
passing through the white wall or escaping the black hole.
To pass through the white wall would be to transgress the
limits of possible experience. To escape the black hole would
be to experience the transcendental ego as the body. Both
escape routes would be condemned a priori by the court
of reason.

Kant's destratified body would have disappeared into
the black hole of this face. This black hole would, in effect,
function as the panoptical eye of the law's face.[53] However,
because the subject itself would now be this eye, it would
be reduced to a mechanism of self-reflective panopticism,
or a constant watching of itself. Kant's sense that obeying
a law is the way to freedom could be said to spring from
this topological location of his empty body. The "I think"
as subject and object of the law would represent the body
as coterminous with the black hole of the law's face. Kant
could be said to attain a type of pure satisfaction solely
in contemplating the matrix which binds him—the white
wall above and the black hole within.

> Two things fill the mind with ever new and increasing
> admiration and awe, the oftener and more steadily
> we reflect on them: the starry heavens above me
> and the moral law within me. . . . The former view
> of a countless multitude of worlds annihilates, as it
> were, my importance as an animal creature, which

must give back to the planet (a mere speck in the universe) the matter from which it came. . . . The latter, on the contrary, infinitely raises my worth as . . . a life independent of all animality and even of the whole world of sense.[54]

Denying his body in order to achieve a sense of self, Kant can take satisfaction only in imagining himself subject to the law.

Or perhaps Kant thinks he can sidestep the Lacanian double-bind by finding a criterion that will enable him to distinguish between autonomously obeying the categorical imperative and heteronomously obeying the Law of the Father. But the problem would be poorly formulated because the very idea of freedom as autonomy locks us into law. Any discipline of resistance that attempts to follow strict laws can only end up being a discipline of domination.

Because he lacks any genealogical understanding of the juridical, Kant cannot question the political stakes of his construal of freedom as law-obeying autonomy. He construes the problem of discipline as a way of overcoming nature, instead of as a way of overcoming political forces of domination. By construing the problem of heteronomy in metaphysical terms rather than in political terms, Kant deceives himself into thinking that he possesses a pure concept of law that need not be genealogically questioned. He gives himself laws to follow in order to make himself free—and right away, he is trapped. His empty body disappears into its black hole. As in the anecdote about the servant who flees for Samara to escape Death only to find that Death has an appointment with him in Samara, Kant seeks to resist heteronomous influence only to fly into a discipline of domination.[55]

But perhaps an alternative model for a Kantian discipline of resistance can be formulated once we have recast the problem of heteronomy in political, rather than in metaphysical, terms.

Chapter Five

The Problem of Heteronomy Recast: How Do You Get Out of a Disciplinary Matrix?

In a disciplinary society, Foucault shows, bodies are frequently isolated from one another and subjected to examination in separate cells in a literal or figurative sense. When Foucault wrote *Discipline and Punish*, he was especially attentive to the techniques of domination that are practiced on such isolated, examined bodies. By the time of the *History of Sexuality* series he began to focus more on the so-called techniques of the self—the various ways in which bodies are trained to train themselves. Techniques of the self work in tandem with techniques of domination, producing docile bodies that are enlisted in their own disciplinary domination.

> Let's say one has to take into account the interaction between those two types of techniques, the point where the technologies of domination of individuals over one another have recourse to processes by which the individual acts upon himself.[1]

However, while *techniques* of the self serve as instruments of further domination, Foucault also came to believe that a certain *care* of the self could serve as a way of avoiding disciplinary domination. He points, in effect, toward the idea of an effective discipline of resistance, although he himself does not characterize such care as being, in itself, an exercise of disciplinary power.[2] Unlike Kant, Foucault cautions that a care-of-the-self ethic could easily end up being just another form of domination—just another technique of the self. This is why he hesitates to articulate it as a general strategy for resistance to disciplinary domination.

Foucault's model treats the mechanism of isolation—the separating of bodies—as a first step in a process, whereby individuals are observed, judged, and trained to productively judge themselves. In other words, on Foucault's analysis, techniques of the self are fostered by the isolating technique of domination. Part of what makes a care-of-the-self ethic ambiguous in its effects is the fact that it remains a practice to be undertaken by individuals—that is, isolated, already disciplined bodies. The idea that we might generate the conditions for a community of resistance—that is, produce the necessary conditions for solidarity—by practicing an individual care of the self is problematic, to say the least.

What Foucault never quite makes explicit is a third group of techniques—ways in which bodies are trained to isolate themselves from one another in the first place, thereby making an individualistic care of the self the only possible activity of resistance. Such practices—which I will call "techniques of mutual betrayal"—are predicated on a certain isolation or potential for isolation already in place. They are devices designed to produce bodies that will be complicitous in a mutual dominating of one another. Despite being isolated from one another—or rather, precisely because they are isolated from one another and as an accentuation of this isolation—disciplined bodies can be trained to discipline not only themselves (through techniques of the self) but one another as well (through techniques of mutual betrayal).

Techniques of mutual betrayal are familiar tactics of disciplinary domination. They operate, for instance, in any divide-and-conquer strategy. Marx's analysis of how structural unemployment keeps wages down provides a classic example. Racism is an effective technique of mutual betrayal. Just to cite a couple of obvious examples, in South Africa, supporters of Apartheid encourage hostilities among different groups of blacks. When India was under British rule, hostilities among Hindus and Muslims were exploited. Bruno Bettelheim describes how concentration camp prisoners in Nazi Germany were trained to discipline their fellow victims. The aim of such techniques is always the same: to break a community of resistance by training its members to betray one another, thereby causing the community to lose its sense of solidarity.

Historically, techniques of mutual betrayal have operated in many different ways. People have been made to betray each other by way of torture, threat, cajoling, reward, and so on. In the disciplinary history that Foucault traces, however, techniques of mutual betrayal begin to take on a special character as methods for training people to *reason themselves* into mutual betrayal. As such, the classic form of a disciplinary technique of mutual betrayal can be found in the model of the prisoner's dilemma, and an importantly different picture of this problem emerges if we look at it in Foucauldian terms rather than, as is usual, in game-theoretic terms.

As is well known, the prisoner's dilemma specifies a set of rules whereby each of two prisoners is given an opportunity to cooperate with the other or to betray the other. If they both cooperate, then their sentence will be shorter than if they both betray each other. However, if one of them cooperates, and the other betrays, the one who betrays wins complete freedom while the other receives a longer sentence. Given these parameters, the *dilemma* arises because it would seem that, no matter what one prisoner does, it is always in the best interest of the other not to cooperate. Because each reasons in the same way, they both end up betraying each other.

The prisoner's dilemma provides a general model of how a *disciplinary* technique of mutual betrayal works. Not only do the victims of disciplinary control become accomplices in their own mutual disciplining, but they do so precisely by attempting to *reason* themselves out of a disciplinary situation. The prisoners are simply informed of "the rules of the game," and then are given an opportunity to extricate themselves from their situation by making a certain "move" in the game.[3]

When the prisoner's dilemma is presented by game theorists, virtually no attention is given to considering the role that power plays in establishing the rules of the "game" in the first place. For game theorists, the parameters of the game are simply defined by the rules, and the sole problem for the theorist is to figure out what would be the "rational" course of action, given that the rules are fixed. Because game-theoretical treatments of the prisoner's dilemma take the only options to be those which amount to playing within the rules—rather than seeking to transform them, refusing to play, and so on—they tend to present the dilemma merely as a rational choice problem, instead of as a problem of how to confront those forms of power that place individuals in these situations in the first place.

Construed in Foucauldian fashion, the prisoner's dilemma might, first of all, be looked at as presenting the prisoners with a technique of domination (imprisonment, and isolation) working in tandem with a technique of the self (encouragement to confess). However, the entire apparatus works only by way of the third technique, which takes the specific form of an appeal to the rationality of the prisoners. The isolated, separated prisoners are given a set of rules which they are told will determine what will happen if any of the four possible scenarios comes up: betrayal/betrayal, betrayal/cooperation, cooperation/ betrayal, and cooperation/cooperation. The rules are set up in such a way as to encourage each prisoner to think that she does better personally to betray her companion— whether that companion betrays her or not. The result is that each prisoner reasons her way to betraying the other, thereby subjecting both herself and her fellow prisoner to a worse situation than would have resulted had each cooperated with the other.

The mutual betrayal that results in the prisoner's dilemma is extracted neither by torture nor by the sort of disciplinary training documented in *Discipline and Punish*. For instance, the isolation of the prisoners is a necessary but not sufficient condition. In this case, mutual betrayal does not result from the mere inculcation of a technique of the self. It results, rather, by way of an appeal to the rationality of bodies who are made to see that the rules of the game favor their becoming agents of domination. Extraction of confession is accomplished, not by the manipulation of the prisoners' bodies, but by a training of their faculty of reason, for only possession of a certain type of rationality will lead the prisoners to their double confession and mutual betrayal.

The specific situation in which bodies are trained to reason themselves into mutual betrayal I will call a "disciplinary matrix."[4] A disciplinary matrix is a social construct with rules that encourage persons to reason themselves into becoming agents of domination. It is oversimplifying only slightly to say that a disciplinary matrix is designed to train bodies to think as do rational-choice theorists in "games" where the "rational" thing to do is to betray everyone else. It is successful in the degree to which it trains its subjects to think that its rules are irresistible, that they must "play the game." The rules become—as they are in game-theoretic problems—inflexible limits that define the scope of possible actions on the part of the prisoners. Thus, the rules of the matrix are, themselves, the most fundamental principles of that form of rationality that the matrix instills in its prisoners.

Hard-core game theorists might object that no training of rationality is necessary. Everyone just naturally possesses the type of rationality that would lock them into the dilemma of the prisoners. However, this is clearly not the case. For one thing, to be aware of the rules of the game is not necessarily to appreciate the nature of the dilemma. For another, some people will naturally take cooperation to be more rational than betrayal, despite a thorough understanding of the stakes. How we come to possess the type of rationality that leads us to believe that the prisoners are faced with a *dilemma* is, in itself, a complex question to which we will return. However, it makes little difference whether the prisoners come to their disciplinary matrix already in full possession of the requisite rational-choice mentality or not. If they do, we can simply conclude that these individuals have already been trained to think like game theorists.

Kant, in effect, argues that pretrained reason—pure practical reason as opposed to empirical—can never lead us to conclude that it would be better to betray others. Even if we reject the Kantian view that there is such a thing as pure—that is, not socially constructed—reason, we can view the categorical imperative as the practical expression of a rationality that refuses to become docile, a rationality that has no "price," to use Kant's term. For this reason, a disciplined adherence to the categorical imperative can never sanction betrayal in the prisoner's dilemma—one cannot universalize a maxim of betrayal.

It is standard in the game-theoretic literature, of course, to note that Kantian ethics offers a type of solution to the prisoner's dilemma which a game-theoretic rationality might not otherwise reach. However, it is important to distinguish between two very different senses of what would count as a "solution" here. For game theorists, a solution is a consistently "winning" strategy, in which this means ending up with the best possible situation given the rules of the game. Morton D. Davis, for example, cites Kantian ethics as specifying this sense of a winning strategy.[5] While Davis is certainly right to note that Kantian ethics recommends a cooperative solution to the prisoner's dilemma, it is, however a solution in a different sense from the one Davis has in mind. Kantian ethics does not tell the prisoners how to win given the rules of the game. Rather, it tells the prisoners to refuse to play the game. We can appreciate the difference by noting that, on Davis' construal, the Kantian player "wins" only if the partner cooperates as well. In fact the prisoner who refuses to betray the partner wins simply by that refusal, regardless of what the partner does. To be sure, if the partner resorts to betrayal, the prisoner loses the game. However, either way, he or she wins by successfully resisting the act of becoming an accomplice of the disciplinary matrix.[6]

Disciplinary matrices destroy the conditions for the possibility of communities of resistance by training persons to reason not as bodies resisting a dominating power, but instead as "rational" players of a game. A certain freedom to reason for themselves is not only conceded, but fostered in a disciplinary matrix. For example, in the prisoner's dilemma, the prisoners are not forced to confess, but are rather encouraged to use their own reason to "freely" decide whether or not they want to confess. Such minimal freedom is important to disciplinary techniques of mutual betrayal. In Kantian terms, we could say that the prisoners are trained to think that they must act in a world where the *summum bonum* is unattainable—that is, a world in which mutual cooperation could never occur. Once we are trained to think that the *summum bonum* cannot be achieved, we are more likely to reason selfishly. For just this reason, Kant reacted with vehemence to writers who argued that humanity could never achieve perfection. In "A Renewed Attempt to Answer the Question: 'Is the Human Race Continually Improving?'" Kant accuses these cynics of dealing in "moral terrorism."[7]

What Kant could not foresee was that the nineteenth- and twentieth-centuries would witness an explosion of disciplinary matrices, complete with arguments about why the *summum bonum* could never be achieved. Such arguments have, of course, been part and parcel of capitalist ideology.[8] Arguments about human nature's being intractable and fixed are common ways in which people are encouraged to think of the rules—or, to go back to Foucault, the "limits of the present"—as eternally fixed. Foucault consistently resisted the view that any rule of the present was fixed— hence, his morally-grounded methodological preference for archaeology over transcendental philosophy.

One of the standard attempts to "solve" the prisoner's dilemma is to imagine alternative conceptions of rationality. Usually, "solve" is meant in the sense of winning the game rather than in the sense of subverting the game. This is the approach taken by both game theorists and discourse ethicists. They seek to articulate a form of rationality that can guard against the narrowly self-centered notion of reason that condemns the prisoners to consistently losing strategies. It is pointed out that reason can be educated.

Prisoners can learn that it is in their mutual best interest to cooperate. (In games that are iterated, of course, this solution is simpler to come by.) In Habermas, the rationality of consensus is stressed, and others have tried to demonstrate the rationality of valuing community. These approaches continue to view the problem as being how to determine the best strategy for playing the game. Habermas's theory of communicative interaction, for instance, is designed to show how rational agents can reach the type of community-conscious rationality that they would need to achieve the most mutually advantageous arrangement of their social institutions.

However, even if Habermas's theory were successful, it would have shown only what the best social arrangement would be, given the present rules of the game—that is, given the limits of the present. Moreover, by remaining within the confines of a theory of rationality, Habermas's strategy threatens to impose a normative standard that will become the rule of its own disciplinary matrix. This, in fact, might be a problem endemic to any juridical approach to social critique.

An alternative to Habermas's approach becomes clearer if we highlight the differences between game-theoretic problems and disciplinary matrix problems. A game-theoretic problem is one which poses a rational construal of a situation defined by a fixed set of rules. The problem is to determine what a rational player should do in such a situation, and find a solution that can be generalized to other situations of the same type. When the prisoner's dilemma is taken to be this sort of problem, there are clear rational procedures for reaching an optimal solution for all players involved. It is also clear that some sort of discourse theory can help the players reach this optimal solution. However, "optimal" remains defined in terms of the parameters of the problem. For instance, in the prisoner's dilemma, the rules of the game specify that there is no possible outcome under which both prisoners would escape punishment completely. Discourse ethics fails to address the more radical question of what it might take to "get out of the present"—that is, to let the prisoners escape punishment entirely.

If we look at the prisoner's dilemma as an example of a disciplinary matrix problem, a different approach becomes possible. A disciplinary matrix problem is first, and foremost, a concrete historical situation calling for a specific response to power formations. The problem is, simply, to escape the matrix itself. To be sure, this may be a regulative ideal that cannot be achieved any more than it could be when the problem is cast in game-theoretic terms. Nonetheless, the strategies called for differ in the two construals of the problem. The most important difference between game-theoretic and disciplinary matrix problems is that the rules of the former are taken to be fixed, while the rules of the latter are capable of being changed. Put otherwise, game-theoretic problems are structural; disciplinary matrix problems are historical. A merely game-theoretic analysis could never yield a truly generalizable solution to a disciplinary matrix problem unless it could anticipate all possible rule changes. This is another reason why no court of reason can provide an adequate strategy for getting out of a disciplinary matrix.

Viewed as a disciplinary matrix problem, the prisoner's dilemma takes on new significance. We can no longer look at it as an abstract problem, but must examine the actual historical circumstances in which it arises. It is no longer a question of what should we do, given that these are the rules of the game, but rather what is to be done, given that we are in this particular situation, in which our alternatives are now said to be delimited by such-and-such rules? In short, the prisoner's dilemma can no longer be looked at as a *game*; any decision to "play the game" would be a losing strategy a priori. The problem faced by the prisoners is not, "How do we play by the rules?," but rather, "How do we defy the rules? How do we subvert them? What can be done to deconstruct the matrix?"

"Playing by the rules" is another way of saying "reasoning in the *proper* way," with *proper* defined by the specific form of rationality that governs the matrix under question. Those who assume that we can only get out of disciplinary matrices by attacking the Enlightenment basically assume that there is only one form of Reason which is an inevitable accomplice of domination. However, this is a flawed strategy for at least two reasons. First, to combat a disciplinary matrix means to confront the specific form of rationality it represents, and this might require opposing its rationality with an alternative model of rationality, (if only for strategic purposes; here we might outline the possibility of a politics based on Pyrrhonian skepticism.) Second—and here, I am invoking a point that is sometimes made by those who defend rational choice theory—we can construe "rational" in an extremely broad way. For instance, any attempt to escape a disciplinary matrix can be considered to be "rational." In this most general sense, we might innocuously concede that there is a certain ineluctability of rationality faced by the prisoners. It is in this light, that we should read Foucault's desire to rescue what he calls the "attitude" of Enlightenment.[9] However, far from providing a solution to the dilemma, to affirm the ineluctability of rationality in this broadest sense merely restates the nature of the problem faced by the prisoners. To ascribe universality to a richer, more determinate concept of rationality—as does Habermas—is, for Foucault, to also simply defend a present form of rationality upon which disciplinary matrices are built. To the extent that the matrices of the present require us to accept as ineluctable this very same form of rationality, those who defend the Enlightenment are accomplices in the techniques for training bodies to think in certain ways. Hence, Foucault's condemnation of "the 'blackmail' of the Enlightenment."[10] To pose as the "guardian of rationality," as Habermas does, is to bar potential escape routes.

While Foucault certainly appreciated the fact that the training of bodies is related to the formation of specific forms of rationality—this, we might say, was his constant theme— he tends not to recognize the degree to which the training of bodies involves a training of *their* rationality. For example, Foucault shows how the discourse on delinquency constitutes a form of rationality that is pivotal in the development of various disciplinary apparatuses. However, these apparatuses are not designed to train prisoners to become theorists of this discourse. In order to create docile bodies, it is not necessary to teach them delinquency theory. While Foucault does highlight some of the ways in which bodies are trained to think,[11] he seems mainly to notice those disciplinary devices that are used to train bodies to react in certain ways rather than to think in certain ways. The training of bodies qua bodies is treated as logically and materially prior to the training of bodies qua reasoning bodies.[12]

However, the logic of disciplinary matrices requires us to recognize that a technique of mutual betrayal involves a training of bodies to think in terms of the form of rationality upon which the matrix itself is predicated. Roughly speaking, we could say that, in the disciplinary matrix of the prisoner's dilemma, it is necessary that the prisoners *learn* the rudiments of game theory. To contrast the training of reasoning bodies with the training of, let us say, *mere* bodies is not to hypostatize reason as something existing over and above bodies. It is merely to acknowledge a difference of mechanism that is peculiar to a prisoner's-dilemma type of disciplinary matrix.

More problematic than the relationship between bodies and reason is the relationship between discipline and reason. With an appreciation of the training of rationality that is part and parcel of techniques of mutual betrayal, we can see why an appeal to the rationality of the prisoners will not necessarily show them a way out of their dilemma. To get out of the matrix will require, instead, a radical rethinking of our familiar distinctions between reason and unreason.

> The relationship between rationalization and excesses of political power is evident. And we should not need to wait for bureaucracy or concentration camps to recognize the existence of such relations. But the problem is: What to do with such an evident fact? Shall we try reason? To my mind, nothing

would be more sterile. First, because the field has nothing to do with guilt or innocence. Second, because it is senseless to refer to reason as the contrary entry to nonreason. Lastly, because such a trial would trap us into playing the arbitrary and boring part of either the irrationalist or the rationalist.[13]

Whether he thought it to be a boring strategy at the time or not, in his first major work, Foucault documented the history of the irrationalist strategy for getting out of a disciplinary matrix. *Madness and Civilization*, in effect, narrates the failure of those whose refusal of a dominant form of rationality made them the principal victims of its domination.[14] Becoming "mad" does not, of itself, free us from the control of disciplinary matrices. On the contrary, the matrices themselves require the production of "madness" as "reason's" other, for, in this way, they enforce the distinction between what counts as reason and what does not. Those who do not want to be locked up are trained to think in accordance with the mode of rationality that the matrix constructs. *Madness and Civilization* can be read as documenting how an irrationalist strategy for getting out of a disciplinary matrix was invented by the matrix itself in order to tighten its hold over both the "mad" and the "normal."

From a game-theoretic perspective, the paradox of the prisoner's dilemma is that following reason leads to an irrational result. The RAND-game theorists who formulated the prisoner's dilemma offer an illustration of how a matrix perpetuates its rationality by constructing its own irrationality. In the face of the Cold War, panicking game-theorists believed that its prisoner's dilemma logic meant that either the United States or the Soviet Union would inevitably reason itself to "betray" the other and launch a preemptive nuclear strike. As a result, many (including Bertrand Russell) called for the United States to launch such a strike before the Soviets could. After the Soviets successfully tested an atomic weapon, it was then argued that we could avoid nuclear Armageddon only if both sides recognized that a type of "MAD-ness"—mutually assured destruction—was preferable to reason. The construction of this MAD-ness seemed to be the only way to keep both sides honest. Of course, this was a tactic for preserving rationality, for assuring the rational result of cooperation. Here, we see "reason's" constructing one type of madness which it keeps at bay in order not to undermine itself. Reason avoids unreason by producing and confining it. Instead of breaking out of the matrix, both sides tighten its control of them. Instead of leading to perpetual peace, the threat of mutually assured destruction accelerates the nuclear arms build-up.

Part of the problem with a simple irrationalist strategy is that it is precisely when reason threatens to become indistinguishable from unreason that bodies get locked up. More importantly, it would be a mistake to associate all reason with the forms of rationality that govern disciplinary matrices. Thus, although Foucault rejects the straightforward Habermasian embracing of reason versus rationalization, he does not simply turn to its symmetrical opposite. From the first, Foucault's archaeological investigations were interested in uncovering multiple rationalities and multiple "knowledges." However because alternative rationalities are viewed as irrational from the perspective of a dominant rationality, to seek multiple rationalities is to seek what the dominant rationality casts as "unreason."

In Habermas's view, Foucault unfairly assumes that all rationality is complicitous with power. Foucault is said "to postulate that *all* discourses (by no means only the modern ones) can be shown to have the character of hidden power and derive from practices of power."[15] If Foucault were right, it would be impossible to formulate a genuinely emancipatory discourse which would free human subjects from those aspects of the life-world which are dominated by forces which curtail human freedom. Any impulse toward a genuinely rational emancipation turns into "nihilistic despair and radical scepticism."[16]

But Habermas's description of Foucault's belief in the inextricability of all discourse with power is misleading. In

Foucault's view, "'Truth' is linked in a circular relation with systems of power which produce and sustain it, and to effects of power which it induces and which extend it. A 'régime' of truth." For one thing, "truth" stands for "what counts as truth" in a given historical situation. In this sense "truth" is also surely determined by dominant powers. Moreover, Foucault immediately notes that, while it would be "a chimera" to separate truth from power, we must seek to "[detach] the power of truth from the forms of hegemony, social, economic and cultural, within which it operates at the present time."[17] To equate power with knowledge is simply to observe that all discourses appear in social contexts which are permeated with power relations, and that all discourses can and do function as instruments of power. However, the power/knowledge equivalence need not commit us to the stronger view that all discourse is oppressive. For one thing, not all power is domination. There is a power of resistance. It is clear that Foucault saw his own discourses as interventions into power struggles. The "specific intellectual" is someone who undertakes microdiscursive interventions into disciplinary matrices.

Foucault's equation of truth with power is meant, in part, to point out that "truths" have real effects in the world and cannot be dismissed as merely superstructural phenomena. While Habermas sometimes seems to believe that emancipation means liberating human subjects from the effects of power entirely, Foucault simply refuses the humanist assumption that emancipation requires getting outside of power altogether. In addition, he warns that what passes for emancipation often conceals its opposite. Thus, Foucault is committed to the ideal of freedom. He is extremely cautious, though, about how to express that commitment.

The problem of how to get out of a disciplinary matrix is not the problem of getting outside of power, but rather the problem of forging a kind of power that will resist techniques of mutual betrayal. For Foucault, the problem of freedom is the problem of how to avoid the heteronomous controls of the present. Where he differs from both

Habermas and Kant is on the question of how to conceive of freedom. Neither the concept of autonomy (still too closely tied to law-giving) nor a negatively defined pure nonheteronomy (the impossible position outside power) suffices. However, Foucault never manages to develop a positive notion of freedom.

Kant also approaches the problem of freedom negatively—that is, from the standpoint of how to avoid a heteronomous determination of the will. For Kant, the greatest threats to freedom are external laws. These laws come roughly under two headings—laws of nature, and laws of the state. Corresponding to these two sorts of law, the problem of freedom has two sides—a metaphysical side, and a political side. How can I act in such a way that my will is not determined by the laws of nature, on the one hand, nor by the laws of the state, on the other?

Kant's practical philosophy is, however, first and foremost, concerned with the metaphysical problem. He wants to show how it is possible for a human will to act without being determined by the laws of nature. To obey the laws of nature—to act on the basis of our inclinations and fears—is to act, Kant argues, in an *undisciplined* way. I cannot be free so long as I remain undisciplined. However, if I practice an ethical ascetics, I will act in a disciplined way. Ethical ascetics is a discipline of resistance to supposed metaphysical impediments to freedom. Kant rushes headlong into his metaphysical discipline of resistance without understanding its political stakes. His inability to distinguish rigorously between a discipline of resistance and a discipline of domination occurs in part because of how he construes the problem of heteronomy—as a way of resisting the laws of nature rather than as a way of resisting social forces of domination.

If Kant can think of discipline only as a discipline of resistance, Foucault's problem is exactly the opposite. He can conceive of discipline only as a principle of domination. Lacking the distinction between the two types of discipline, Foucault was unable to clarify the difference between a technique of the self and an effective care of the self. For this reason, too, he could think of ethical judgments only as further oppressive limits of the present. In Foucault's eyes, anyone who seeks to construct a Kantian ethical theory—such as Habermas—is simply trying to lock us into a normative straitjacket.

Of course, Habermas construes emancipation differently from the way in which Kant does. Habermas does not define freedom in terms of following laws, and he is aware that apparent liberation can, in fact, be its opposite. By siding with reason against unreason as simple alternatives, however, Habermas risks reinforcing an essential underpinning of disciplinary matrices. Even if Habermas is right to maintain that a certain type of rationality is ineluctable for human agents, we must be cautious in subjecting what we might call the "unreason option" to disciplinary action. By contrast, Foucault's insistence on thinking of "unreason" as a legitimate tactical refusal of disciplinary control is an attempt to prevent a matrix from tightening an inexorable grip on subjects who can reason only in a certain way. As the prisoner's dilemma illustrates, only a radical rethinking of the relationship between reason and unreason can get us out of a disciplinary matrix.

The problem of how to get out of a disciplinary matrix is precisely the same as Deleuze's and Guattari's problem of how to get out of a black hole. The white-wall/black-hole system that traps Kant is the perfect disciplinary matrix, as seen in terms of its structural aims of rule formation and creation of docile bodies. Disciplinary matrices perform the two functions to which Deleuze and Guattari refer as "signifiance" and "subjectification." A disciplinary matrix constructs rules which determine the significance of any moves that its disciplined subjects might make. In so doing, it also simultaneously trains these subjects to reason in accordance with these rules. These rules are part of the discursive regime. They are a matrix's "truths." Reason must be trained—disciplined—not to violate the law of signifiance, and trained by culture to construct the law of a matrix.

Perhaps a way out of its black hole would be possible for the Kantian subject if it could construct itself to be otherwise—specifically, as something like a transcendental body. The idea of a transcendental body would be the idea of a person reduced, neither to an abstract transcendental subject that is separate from its body and at war with its desires, nor to an empirical body that is a mere subject of positivistic disciplinary control. Samuel Todes suggests one way in which Kant's theory of the constitution of the subject might be nudged in this direction. Kant believes we can only represent our self-activity as the empty "I think," but, as Todes points out, we can locate Kantian self-activity in "the felt unity of our active body."[18] Mark Poster suggests that it was just this element in Kant that Foucault sought to develop.

> Foucault extracts from the Enlightenment—and from Kant in particular—the problematic of the constitution of the self, relating this to Kant's "dare to know." . . . On this formulation rests the achievement of Kant that Foucault would emulate.[19]

For Kant, this problematic can only be thematized in terms of the transcendental ego that is at war with its body. Hence, he cannot get out of his black hole. One way of characterizing Kant's problem is to say that he views the transcendental and the empirical as radically separate. The transcendental ego cannot identify itself with the empirical body. Seeking to correct this problem, Deleuze contrasts Kant's transcendental idealism with what he calls a "transcendental empiricism."[20] As Ronald Bogue describes this hybrid,

> Deleuze's method is empirical because its object is experience. . . . It is transcendental because empirical principles always . . . require a transcendental analysis of their implicit condition or presupposition.[21]

For Kant, the transcendental is always "prior" to experience. For Deleuze, by contrast, the transcendental is itself made possible by experience.

However, if Kant errs in viewing the transcendental and the empirical as diametrically opposed, so does Foucault.

This produces a different sort of problem. We have seen Habermas suggesting that Foucault cannot avoid recourse to the transcendental altogether. Terms such as *discursive regime, power,* and *discipline* all function as the very limiting terms that Foucault thought he could get rid of. To be sure, we might call some of these historical parameters rather than absolute limits—*bio-power* and *discipline* for instance. But others—such as *discursive regime, episteme,* and *power*—are terms of which the scope of application should, in principle, be all historical periods.

In his reading of Foucault, Deleuze shows how to read power as a type of transcendental element. For Deleuze, one of the central Foucauldian problems is to specify how the *visible*—that which can be observed—relates to the *articulable*— that which can be judged. In *The Archaeology of Knowledge,* Deleuze notes, Foucault tries to explain this relation by characterizing the articulable as a map that organizes the visible. In other words, judgment would function as a way of mapping that which is judged.[22] The problem is that, while the articulable and the visible are heterogeneous, for the one to apply to the other they must be commensurable.[23] Deleuze notes the striking parallel between this Foucauldian problem of relating the articulable to the visible, and Kant's comparable problem of relating the categories to the sensory manifold. Kant, of course, could solve this problem only by invoking a mediating third term—the *schemata.*

> Kant had already undergone a similar adventure: the spontaneity of understanding did not exert its determination of the receptivity of intuition without the latter continuing to contrast its form of the determinable with that of determination. Kant therefore had to invoke a third agency beyond the two forms that was essentially "mysterious" and capable of taking account of their coadaptation as Truth. This was the *schema* of imagination.[24]

Foucault ends up with a similar solution:

> Even Foucault needs a third agency to coadapt the determinable and determination, the visible and the

articulable, the receptivity of light and the spontaneity of language, operating either beyond or this
side of the two forms.[25]

On Deleuze's reading, it was not until Foucault wrote
Discipline and Punish that he could say how the visible and
the articulable worked together. It is *power* which links the
visible and the articulable in the functioning of discursive
practices. Further drawing out the Kant/Foucault connection, Deleuze calls this Foucauldian schematism a
"diagrammaticism."

Foucault's diagrammaticism, that is to say the
presentation of pure relations between forces or the
transmission of pure particular features, is therefore
the analogue of Kantian schematicism: it is this that
ensures the relation from which knowledge flows,
between the two irreducible forms of spontaneity
and receptivity.[26]

On this model, power functions as a type of transcendental condition for the functioning of discursive mechanisms. Of course, Foucault rejects such a view because he
believes that the transcendental can only yield absolute
limits. However, what if, taking a cue from Deleuze, we
view the transcendental as having a history? Is it possible
to view transcendental limits as contingent parameters that
are nonetheless transcendental? In other words, can we view
transcendental limits as conditions for the possibility of
history which are nonetheless themselves generated
historically?

Power has a history—it emerges as disciplinary power
or bio-power only in the modern world. Yet in all historical
periods, there is some form of power at work, organizing
the way in which "words and things" are constructed.
In one sense, power is an absolute limit. However, because
what power *is* differs in different historical situations,
any specific form of power is a contingent parameter. To
view the transcendental as historical is, perhaps, simply
to posit, as an absolute limit, the presence of some sort
of contingent limits.[27]

Foucault's imperative to escape the limits of the present is, in itself, a type of transcendental prescription. Were we to reject the transcendental altogether, would we not have to treat this prescription as just another type of limit—as just another "Thou shalt" for Zarathustra's lion to slay? To be sure, the present's conditions are contingent parameters, but the Foucauldian imperative would presumably apply to *every* present.

It is here that a revised version of Kantian ethics might help us. Kant's failed discipline of resistance stems from his separation of the transcendental and the empirical. However, what might it be like from a more Deleuzian standpoint? Is it possible to retain the transcendental moment that gives Kantian ethics a strategy for freedom without accepting his conclusion that freedom means autonomy—that freedom means obeying law? Is it possible to recast the categorical imperative as a general *strategy* for forming communities of resistance rather than as a law that we must blindly give ourselves to follow regardless of historical circumstance? Construed in this way, a revised Kantian ethics might provide just what Foucauldian thought needs—that is, a transcendental condition for the possibility of resisting techniques of mutual betrayal.

It is Kant, after all, who gives us an answer to the question of how to get out of a disciplinary matrix, for this question is essentially the same as the question of how to avoid heteronomy in any form. Kant's answer is: Always act in accordance with a maxim that you could will be to universal. This is another way of saying, never succumb to techniques of mutual betrayal. To be sure, Kant did not know how to think of the categorical imperative as a Foucauldian strategy of resistance. But can we rewrite it in this way?

Chapter Six

From Principles to Strategies:
A "B Edition" of Kant's Second *Critique*

To recast the categorical imperative as the basis for Foucauldian ethics, it is necessary to steer it away from the law, for it is Kant's rigidly juridical construal of the problem of freedom which twists his attempted discipline of resistance into a discipline of domination. The problem, then, is to imagine what a nonjuridical version of Kantian ethical theory might look like. In this chapter I will show how such an approach could retain some of Kant's basic insights concerning the centrality of the categorical imperative to ethical considerations without locking us into the rigid, ahistorical normative stance of his full-blown moral theory. Instead of viewing the categorical imperative as an a priori *law*, I will try to show how it might be reworked as a general *strategy*, the application of which, in historically specific situations, calls for actions the generalizability of which is limited by relevant, contingent, and genealogically articulated features of these situations. Recast in this way, the categorical imperative could provide Foucauldian critique with an ethical basis for a politics of resistance without giving up the Foucauldian insistence on treating all limits as contingent. Such a position, moreover, would escape the merely relativistic because it would posit the categorical imperative as a *transcendental* strategy of which the specific form would, nonetheless, remain historically contingent.

In Kant's moral philosophy, the problem of freedom is not framed in genealogical terms at all. Because Kant thinks that all humans possess a sort of transhistorical rationality which provides us with a pure idea of freedom, he is unable to question the historical origins and social constitution of this idea. As we have seen, moreover, for Kant the problem of heteronomy is primarily a metaphysical problem. It is only in a secondary—and derivative—sense that Kant wrestles with the social and political impediments to freedom. Kant's juridical construal of reason leads to the conclusion that all human action is necessarily governed by law. Hence, the central task of the second *Critique* is merely to determine whether it is possible for a person to give himself or herself a law to follow instead of always following the external laws of nature. Viewed in the context of this juridically articulated metaphysical problematic, Kant could only construe the categorical imperative as a pure law to be strictly obeyed. Not only the categorical imperative, but also the practical principles Kant claims to derive from it, function as absolute limits which must be acknowledged regardless of social circumstances.

However, if we take on the Kantian problematic from a genealogically oriented perspective, then prior to any metaphysical questions that might come up are questions that concern a historically situated discourse on "freedom."[1] Instead of positing a pure idea of freedom, we can only retrieve or construct historically situated notions of freedom. This does not mean, however, that we must abandon the transcendental move which would ascribe to notions of freedom a constitutive role in framing our practical experience. We can posit the ideal of freedom as transcendental while simultaneously acknowledging that its specific form is determined by historical circumstance. Put otherwise, there is nothing to preclude the possibility that transcendental limits have a history that we must approach genealogically. Building on Foucault's genealogy of our present disciplinary age, we can articulate an ideal of freedom today in terms of the problem of how to get out of a disciplinary matrix. Enriched with genealogical content, the categorical imperative can be interpreted as saying, "Always act in accordance with a strategy for resisting disciplinary domination that could be willed to become a general strategy for everyone to adopt." Or, put otherwise, "Resist techniques of mutual betrayal."

As we saw in chapter five, one does not necessarily "win" the prisoner's dilemma by adopting the categorical imperative as one's guiding strategy—at least not when the dilemma is construed in game-theoretic terms. However, when viewed as a disciplinary matrix problem, the prisoner's dilemma requires a strategy for refusing to play its game. From this perspective, the categorical imperative recommends the only strategy that "wins" consistently by putting dignity above docility. It says, "Have no price. Do not be made complicitous with a discipline of domination no matter what the stakes of the game."

Those who favor some sort of Kantian ethics but recognize problems with Kant's refusal to countenance exceptions to general rules have tried to see whether the categorical imperative could be shown to allow for greater flexibility than Kant's own development of it would allow. For Kant, there are certain absolute moral principles which immediately follow from the categorical imperative and which ought to be followed regardless of the particular circumstances in which we find ourselves. Most commentators have assumed that this is the only way of drawing out the implications of the categorical imperative. Those who seek to reform Kantian ethics to make it more responsive to the complexities of particular circumstances usually try to rewrite the categorical imperative in one way or another.[2] But the excessive inflexibility problem does not lie with the categorical imperative itself, but rather with how Kant thinks through its implications. Here, I will suggest an alternative way of thinking through these implications. Instead of deriving a Kantian principled morality from the categorical imperative, I want to show how we might derive from it a Foucauldian strategic politics.

Foucault, of course, does not *want* a generalizable ethical or political strategy. In rejecting the view that there are global power struggles, he, in effect, limits the scope of practical reasoning to local conditions. The underlying logic of his position seems to be based on a spatial model of separate zones of power that intersect but do not coincide. To be sure, this metaphor is not to be taken literally. In one and the same place, we find ourselves engaged in struggles of gender, race, class, etc. However, any particular sphere of power relations constitutes a unique "site" that cannot be reduced to any other. Foucault treats diverse relations of power as if they occupied heterogeneous positions. It is just this heterogeneity that leads him to conclude that struggle must always take on the character of a limited microintervention. Foucault's notion of *micropolitics* is meant to specify the limited scope of any tactics of resistance to domination.

Yet, even if we were to grant Foucault the spatial heterogeneity of relations of power, there is a temporal continuity in the history of specific fields of power which requires a type of "global" strategizing across time. For instance, the fact that the rules of a disciplinary matrix problem are always capable of changing—one of the crucial features that distinguishes it from a game-theoretic problem—requires that we intervene in a way that will take into account any possible future permutations of the matrix. As Jean-François Lyotard reminds us, any change in the rules of a game—or a matrix—can radically change the game or matrix under question.[3] In turn this can also mean a redrawing of the map which delineates heterogeneous spheres of power relations. The diachronic instability of disciplinary matrices should suggest that we cannot treat them merely as stable or local formations. Moreover, lacking a full genealogy of the present, we cannot assume that, at any given moment in time, we know where the boundaries of one matrix stops and another one begins. We must maximize our purview accordingly if we are to understand what sort of intervention is appropriate for what we take to be the local struggle under question. The point I want to make is that, even if Foucault were right to suggest that we can only engage in microstruggles, we cannot resort to momentary tactics without formulating a general strategy that will take into account other microstruggles as well. It would be a mistake, for instance, to treat particular gender struggles as having nothing to do with particular class struggles. Resistance requires strategy—and strategy is already a step beyond a merely nominalistic micropolitics.

To be sure, strategies must be situation-specific, but they also require a degree of universalizability that will give them continuing applicability in an on-going struggle. Foucauldian politics emphasizes the particularity of microstruggles, while Kantian ethics emphasizes universalizability. Can we put these together in some way? Can we articulate a Foucauldian, strategic version of the categorical imperative?

Those who reject the strictness and formalism of Kantian ethics typically lay the blame on the categorical imperative itself, rather than on the principles which Kant claims to deduce from it. However, what is really being objected to in such criticisms is not the categorical imperative itself, but these derivative principles.[4] For instance, what gets Kant into trouble in the notorious problem of "can you ever lie to the rapist," is not the categorical imperative per se, but the rigid principle which forbids us from ever lying. Viewed from a Kantian perspective, the positing of such rigid principles seems to be an unavoidable implication of the categorical imperative. After all, how else could we get from an empty practical law to concrete prescriptions for action without positing some set of absolutely binding moral principles that have the form of law as well as tell us specifically what to do?

It is important, however, to distinguish between what the categorical imperative tells us and what it does not tell us. It tells us only one thing—to act in accordance with maxims that we could will everyone to follow. However, there are at least two important things which it does not tell us. First, it does not—at least when taken by itself— tell us which maxims to adopt. Second—and more importantly—it does not tell us how to determine whether or not we judge correctly when we decide that a certain maxim is capable of being universally followed. Kant thought it to be immediately obvious which maxims could and which could not be willed to become universal. In some relatively unproblematic cases, his confidence seems warranted. It seems certain, for example, that we cannot will to become universal a maxim that would recommend indiscriminate killing. However, not every case is so easy. Can we will a world in which everyone would decline to aid their neighbors? Not everyone agrees on whether or not Kant is right to reply in the negative to this question.[5]

To determine whether a maxim is consistent with the categorical imperative might seem exactly the same as to determine whether its symmetrical opposite is inconsistent with it. So, for example, if a maxim that recommends killing is inconsistent when generalized over all situations, it might seem fair to conclude that a maxim that recommends against killing in all situations must be consistent with the categorical imperative. Still, is such symmetry preserved in all cases? Take, for instance, Kant's favorite example—a maxim that bids one to lie. Suppose we grant Kant the conclusion that no rational agent could will a world in which lying would be universal. Does it necessarily follow that a maxim which would bid us never to lie is, therefore, automatically consistent with the categorical imperative? When cases in which it clearly seems wrong to tell the truth are raised against Kant, they are raised as objections to the rigidity of the categorical imperative. However, the categorical imperative itself should provide us with the resources to see that it would be wrong, for instance, to assist a rapist by telling him the truth. Surely we cannot universalize a maxim that would bid us to aid those who seek to treat others merely as means.

The problem is that Kant gives us no room to maneuver at this point. Having demonstrated that we cannot universalize a maxim that recommends indiscriminate lying, he concludes that we must adopt the maxim that recommends indiscriminate truth-telling. He has left himself no room to change his maxims as his moral experience broadens. However, is this the fault of the categorical imperative? Or is it Kant's fault for assuming that we can tell a priori which specific maxims must be universalized? Put otherwise, we could say that Kant errs by hastily affirming the "CI consistency" of a maxim simply on the basis of having demonstrated the "CI inconsistency" of its symmetrical opposite. That is, he has decided that we can will a world in which no one ever lies simply on the basis of his realization that we cannot will a world in which everyone always lies. Yet he gives us no reason to think that our choices must be limited to this either/or set of options.

At issue here is a question of the narrowness and broadness of maxims.[6] Assuming that we cannot universalize the broad maxim that sanctions indiscriminate lying, why are we then prohibited from considering whether a somewhat narrower maxim—one that sanctions lying under certain specific circumstances—might be CI-consistent? When is a maxim too narrowly constructed, and when is it too broadly constructed? There are many different maxims that we might be following were we to decide to lie to a rapist. We might be following a maxim which bids us to lie when it is to our convenience, and certainly this maxim does not seem to be CI-consistent. However, we might instead be following a maxim which bids us to lie only to those who would use our truth-telling to treat someone merely as a means. On the face of it, this maxim certainly seems universalizable.

The obvious problem with this approach, of course, is that we can end up construing all of our actions in accordance with maxims that are so narrow as to be CI-consistent in a trivial sense. The categorical imperative would be useless if it did not show us how to determine when we have constructed our maxims too narrowly. Yet, why not also acknowledge that there is a comparable problem with construing maxims too broadly? Kant assumes that the categorical imperative allows for only the broadest construction of maxims, but perhaps we can recast the categorical imperative in such a way as to allow *experience* to teach us when maxims that, at one time, seemed to be CI-consistent are, in fact, inconsistent because they have been constructed either too narrowly or too broadly.

In the introduction to the second *Critique*, Kant argues that we must consider the faculties of reason, understanding, and sensibility in inverse order from that followed in the first *Critique.*

> Because it is still pure reason, the knowledge of which here underlies its practical use, the organization of the *Critique of Practical Reason* must conform, in its general outline, to that of the critique of speculative reason. . . . Only the order in the subdivision of the Analytic will be the reverse of that in the critique of speculative reason. For in the present work we begin with principles and proceed to concepts, and only then, if possible, go on to the senses, while in the study of speculative reason we had to start with the senses and end with principles. . . . The reason for this lies in the fact that here we have to deal with a will and to consider reason not in relation to objects but in relation to this will and its causality. The principles of the empirically unconditioned causality must come first.[7]

Kant adopts a top-down model for thinking through the categorical imperative, rather than a bottom-up model. Instead of working up from experience (faculty of sensibility) to transcendental guidelines for action (faculties of understanding and reason), Kant thinks he must specify a pure transcendental guideline which cannot be worked up from experience. The reason for this approach is that Kant seeks to determine whether or not pure reason can be practical.[8] This means not merely establishing the transcendental character of the categorical imperative, but also establishing its pure pedigree. Once this is accomplished, it then becomes necessary to work down from the categorical imperative to experience. This requires a positing of the practical rules that Kant believes must necessarily follow.

The problem, of course, is that the categorical imperative, as Kant formulates it, is supposed to be pure and thus devoid of any content. By itself, it would be useless as a guide to action. What we need is some intermediary that would bridge the gap between the contentless categorical imperative and our content-rich experiences. The subjective principles of reason that we can adopt—our maxims—can play this role in one respect—that of providing potential content that is empirically rich for the empirically contentless categorical imperative. However, as merely subjective principles, maxims cannot play the type of pure mediating role that, for example, the schemata play in mediating between the categories and the pure forms of intuition. If we are to demonstrate that pure practical reason can be practical, we must show that reason can determine the will in terms of merely objective principles. If the categorical imperative does not suffice in this regard, neither can our maxims.

For Kant, only pure practical principles—objective principles (laws) as opposed to subjective principles (maxims)—can serve the pure mediating role that will enable pure reason to inform the will on how to act in particular circumstances. Yet, are there such things? Or do all practical rules divide into the contentless (categorical imperative) and the subjective (maxims)? Put otherwise, are there any content-rich objective practical principles? Or, as Lewis White Beck formulates the question, "Are there any fundamental principles in the strict sense of a priori synthetic propositions which contain a determination of the will; and, if so, what are they?"[9]

Beck notes the difficulty that Kant has with trying to rigorously maintain the distinction between maxims and principles.[10] He characterizes Kantian ethics as providing a tripartite distinction among maxims, laws, and laws that are also maxims.[11] The problem, in Kant's eyes, is to see whether there are laws that can also serve us as maxims. In other words, can the categorical imperative yield practical principles that are, in some sense, both objective and subjective?

Kant, of course, will answer this question in the negative. Maxims all have their sources in the lower faculty of desire and are thus exclusively subjective. All maxims arise from the principle of happiness, which can never give rise to "maxims which are competent to be laws of the will."[12] The search for objective practical principles will have to turn elsewhere.

In his writings on moral education, Kant emphasizes the role that experience plays in teaching us moral lessons. On the face of it, it would seem that any genetic account of moral education introduces a historical element that undercuts Kant's claim to have discovered "ready-made" practical principles. However, Kant would deny this, by distinguishing between two sorts of origin. For instance, in the first *Critique*, he suggests that there is no contradiction in recognizing that experience must occasion the use of concepts which are, nonetheless, a priori. In a similar way, moral education merely provides an occasion for the cultivation of reason's innate talent. There is no problem with experience's preparing us to judge, provided that it is still reason—not experience—that is rendering judgment. Under no circumstances can experience correct a judgment made by practical reason. This is also why only the broadest of rules can count for Kant as content for the categorical imperative. The only thing that might lead us to narrow the scope of a rule would be experience, whose coauthority in judging with reason would, thereby, undermine the a priori pretensions of Kantian morality. For Kant, therefore, the only way of bridging the gap between the categorical imperative and experience is to posit principles of practical reason which function as the "schemata" of moral judgment. The rigidity of Kant's ethics comes, not from the categorical imperative itself, but from the way in which it is schematized—that is in terms of these juridical principles.

The parallel between pure practical principles and the schematism of the first *Critique* can be carried a step further. In both cases, Kant seeks to show how the world must be made to conform with the dictates of the court of reason. The only way this can be accomplished is by subjecting the temporal to laws. In *Kant and the Problem of Metaphysics,* Heidegger shows the centrality of the schematism in Kant. He also attempts to show how Kant broached, but shrank back from, an appreciation of the centrality of the faculty of imagination in human experience. From the first edition to the second edition of the *Critique*, Heidegger notes, Kant shifted the power of imagination from being an independent faculty of its own to being a "function of the understanding."[13] Heidegger asks, "Why did Kant shrink back from the transcendental power of imagination?"[14] He answers this question by suggesting that Kant saw—but did not know how to think through—the fact that the imagination could provide the ground for an ontology of human finitude. Heidegger attempts to retrieve this ground by emphasizing the role that temporality plays as the horizon of human finitude. The schemata are ways in which the imagination synthesizes time. Taking the schematizing work of the imagination to be the central ground of human ontology in Kant, Heidegger sees his own effort at constructing a fundamental ontology as a continuation of the Kantian project of critique.

By pointing to the centrality of the schematism in Kant, Heidegger provides an important clue for a metadeductive inquiry into the juridical model of Kantian critique. The court of reason issues laws that must be imposed on the world in both the first and second *Critiques*. In the latter, these laws—the pure practical principles—function as the "schemata" that the subject must obey. As with the schemata of the first *Critique*, these principles also function as ways of ordering time—as ways of subjecting time to laws. This, of course, is precisely what we saw at work in Kant's care of the self: all becomings must be transformed into law-governed moments.

Here, we can draw on Deleuze's analysis of the schematizing function of power for Foucault to clarify the relationship between law and domination in Kant's care of the self. Kant's disciplinary regimen is the mediating term that enables him to relate his visible body to his articulable body. Specifically, his care of the self renders possible a constant normalizing judgment. In giving himself strict laws to follow, Kant undertakes to construct the most normalized body on the planet, a norm for all. Thus, when he writes, "The Conflict of the Philosophy Faculty with the Faculty of Medicine"—his-care-of-the-self primer—he puts his own life forth as the healthiest example of a human being. Here, we might also recall Kant's exclamation when he makes himself into a cocoon—"Is it possible to imagine a human being healthier"—that is more normalized—"than I?" Keeping in mind Foucault's rejection of the juridical model of power, if we are to free the Kantian subject from the law, we must resist the schematizing tyranny of his discipline of domination.

Once again, we come up against the need to distinguish between the two sorts of discipline—a discipline of resistance and a discipline of domination. In general, discipline functions precisely as a way of schematizing time. The problem, then, is to figure out how to schematize time in a way that resists domination. This is precisely what a Foucauldian care-of-the-self ethic points to—the possibility of a different sort of exercise of disciplinary power. Had Heidegger formulated the problem of human finitude as a problem of power rather than as a problem of fundamental ontology—that is had he read Foucault—*Kant and the Problem of Metaphysics* might have been written as *Kant and the Problem of Discipline*.

Obviously, a parallel can be drawn between the schematizing role of discipline in Kant's care of the self and the schematizing role played by practical principles in his moral theory. What further links them are features of disciplinary power that close off rather than open up possibilities for communities of resistance. We have seen how, on Foucault's analysis, disciplinary power exerts its control by isolating bodies. Precisely the same sort of isolation is brought about in Kant's care of the self and in his moral theory because, in both cases, he locks his body in a regimen that cuts it off from the rest of the world. To be sure, the categorical imperative provides the basis for a way out of disciplinary matrices, but only if we interpret it in the historically sensitive way which I have outlined. So long as we maintain the pretense that it is a pure principle, we are unable to derive anything from it other than strategically inflexible rules that must be dogmatically followed in all circumstances.

If we give up Kant's view that there is such a thing as a pure version of the categorical imperative, we can then develop a bottom-up approach to formulating it, and a kind of back-and-forth approach to deriving more specific schematizing strategies from it. We could give up the Kantian ideal of formulating empirically rich rules for conduct in some sort of a priori manner while, nonetheless, retaining the categorical imperative as a transcendental— but not pure—strategy which would bid us to consider whether our contingent subjective maxims can be willed to become universal. Moreover, instead of insisting that reason alone is entitled to test the universalizability of a maxim, we could view experience as providing the basis for a reflective judging—and revising—of our maxims. Instead of requiring us to adopt pure principles that must be determinately applied to experience, the categorical imperative—itself still transcendental, but also genealogically formulated—could be construed as asking us to adopt empirical strategies that we arrive at by way of reflection.

The first thing to notice about such a revised version of Kantian ethics is that it compels us, when constructing our maxims, to take seriously the question of how to determine the optimal middle ground between narrowness and broadness. The second thing to notice is that empirical experience must play an important role in answering this question. This is not to say that we must forsake deontological ethics in favor of some sort of consequentialism. On the contrary, the sole determiner of the rightness or wrongness of an action will still be—in good Kantian fashion—whether the maxim that we take to sanction the action could be willed to be universal or not. In evaluating maxims, we look to the categorical imperative, but we must also evaluate the adequacy of our formulation of the categorical imperative by looking to experience.

Reflective judgment would play a crucial role in the on-going process of maxim formation and maxim application in praxis. Whenever we find ourselves in some particular situation in which we have to choose between competing courses of action, we must consider what various possible maxims we might be construed as following were we to act in a particular way. We would seek to act in accordance with a maxim that could become universal, but we have no a priori principle that could tell us what maxim this would be.

Suppose we are in our first-ever situation in which we consider telling a lie. We ask ourself if we could will indiscriminate lying to become universal, and we conclude that we cannot. Assuming that our practical reasoning were to stop there, we might accordingly decide not to lie. Later, we perhaps realize that, by not lying in some particular situations, we risk being an accessory to a technique of mutual betrayal. Now we must go back and consider whether the strategy that we had earlier adopted was too broad. Perhaps we should have adopted a strategy that would bid us to lie only when failure to lie would result in someone being treated merely as a means. It is easy to see where all this leads—practical experience becomes a matter of seeking some sort of "reflective equilibrium" between the presupposed strategies that inform our actions and the experiences that lead us to revise these strategies. What we are left with, in effect, is a fallibilistic version of Kantian ethics.

In certain situations, it will be difficult to specify exactly what the categorical imperative recommends. This would be true in any case in which we can find no way out of a disciplinary matrix. William Styron's novel *Sophie's Choice* gives us an example of such a situation.[15] Sophie is told she must choose which of her two children is to remain free and which is to go to a Nazi concentration camp. If she declines to choose, she is informed that both children will be taken to the camp. This is a classic example of a disciplinary matrix problem, in which a victim of disciplinary control is asked to reason herself into complicity with the domination of herself and others.

We can highlight certain differences between strict Kantian ethics and the version which I am developing here by contrasting alternative ways of assessing Sophie's various options. For Kant, it is clear that Sophie should not condemn one child as a means to helping the other. Of course, if she follows this advice, her inaction will lead to the condemning of both children. However, in Kant's view, the consequences of an action are irrelevant for determining the worth of an action. Thus, Sophie would be wrong to choose simply because she could save one child. (This is one of those situations in which Kantian ethics reasons to a different conclusion from utilitarian ethics.)

Construing the categorical imperative as a transcendental strategy, the consequences of an action would matter, (although not because we adopt a utilitarian calculus). If we construe the categorical imperative as bidding us to resist techniques of mutual betrayal, then it would advise Sophie to consider which course of action is most likely to prevent her from becoming an agent of domination, but what course of action is this? On the face of things, it would seem as if Sophie's best choice would be to avoid complicity by declining to make a choice. She would "exit" the matrix by refusing to play by the rules of its game. However, what makes the disciplinary matrix represented here so constricting is that Sophie seems unable to extricate herself from it without her action functioning as a "move" in its game. Even if she decides not to choose between her children, she will, thereby, be making another type of choice, the consequences of which will be determined by the rules of the matrix. What the categorical imperative would recommend here is, therefore, difficult to say because there seems to be no way of completing avoiding this matrix's technique of mutual betrayal. Sophie might try to minimize the effects of domination (perhaps by deciding to save one child), or to minimize her complicity with the matrix (perhaps by not choosing either child).

Still, when the categorical imperative is reformulated as a transcendental strategy, it is a tool with much greater flexibility for resisting the forces that attempt to break communities of resistance. The shortcomings of Kant's moral philosophy should not be blamed on the categorical imperative itself, but rather on how Kant thought through its implications. It is important to see, moreover, that where Kant went wrong was to construe the categorical imperative as a law-giving principle rather than as a matrix-resisting strategy. Whether all juridically modeled ethics are incapable of distinguishing carefully between a discipline of resistance and a discipline of domination is a question that a metadeductive inquiry should further address. Because he lacks the metadeductive means for questioning his own juridical model, Kant unquestioningly brings the problem of heteronomy within the confines of the court, and the court always yields the same verdict—You must obey law. Whether the problem of freedom is framed in metaphysical terms (freedom from the laws of nature) or political terms (freedom from state control), the court's solution is to legislate a type of counterlaw. But this amounts to little more than attempting to construct one's own disciplinary matrix.

On Nietzsche's reading, Kant has a sort of will-to-docility which leads him to construct an ethical theory based on obedience to law.[16] It is on the basis of this Nietzschean reading that both Lacan and Deleuze call attention to the surreptitious pleasure which Kant seems to take in obeying the law. For Kant, it would seem, the only "solution" to the trap of disciplinary matrices is to embrace the absence of a solution—to invest one's desire in the matrix itself. To take pleasure in obeying the moral law would be a way of cutting one's losses, reaping some small reward in exchange for voluntarily losing.

On my reading, however, this result is an unfortunate consequence of Kant's failure to distinguish rigorously between a discipline of resistance and a discipline of domination, rather than the result of a type of innate will-to-docility. Kant went wrong because he construed the problem of freedom—and the problem of resistance—on a juridical model.

However, to reject the juridical is not to give up the ideal of a categorical imperative of the right sort. In fact, from Nietzsche to Foucault, we also see an attempt to formulate an alternative version of a Kantian ethic. Deleuze, for instance, detects a type of categorical imperative in Nietzsche. "Whatever you will, will it in such a way that you also will its eternal return."[17] The work of Deleuze and Guattari can also be read as putting forth something like a transcendental strategy for resisting disciplinary matrices. Thus, we find them offering such genealogically enriched imperatives as:

> Make rhizomes, not roots, never plant! Don't sow, grow offshoots! Don't be one or multiple, be multiplicities! Run lines, never plot a point! Speed turns the point into a line! Be quick, even when standing still![18]

Foucault, in his introduction to *Anti-Oedipus*, also extracts several formulations of a categorical imperative from their work.

> This art of living counter to all forms of fascism, whether already present or impending, carries with it *a certain number of essential principles* which I would summarize . . . if I were to make this great book into a manual or guide to everyday life.[19]

Foucault goes on to list several such "principles," any of which could function as a strategic maxim—"Free political action from all unitary and totalizing paranoia. . . . Do not use thought to ground a political practice in Truth. . . . Do not become enamored of power."[20]

Kant obviously believes that we can only interpret the categorical imperative as giving us laws to follow. As such, he was a victim of a dominating discipline of reason. Put otherwise, he saw ethical problems from a game-theoretic standpoint. However, it is clear how the categorical imperative can be turned into something radically different—a Deleuzian formula which, to use Foucault's word, resists "fascism" by conducting radical politics outside the court of reason.

If the categorical imperative is reinterpreted as a general strategy for subverting disciplinary matrices, it can serve as the basis for a very different sort of ethic from the one which Kant actually develops. Instead of issuing a set of decrees through the court of reason, the categorical imperative becomes, instead, a strategy for undermining those mechanisms that exercise a discipline of domination over bodies. Although the categorical imperative remains a transcendental strategy, it is one with content which is always supplied by genealogy.

The dialectic between the genealogical and transcendental reflections which construct a situated categorical imperative is a precarious one, to be sure. Were we to reject the transcendental move completely, we would be left— as Fraser and Habermas suggest—without the needed ethical basis for praxis. A parallel problem would arise were we to seek some sort of pure transcendental formula for a categorical imperative that could apply to all historical situations. As with Kant's own ethics, we would thereby risk ending up with an abstract and strategically inflexible formalism.

A historically mediated categorical imperative which bids us to resist techniques of mutual betrayal seems to avoid both extremes. However, it is only a provisional statement based on our genealogical understanding of present power formations. Actual praxis and reflection will require its continual transcendental reformulation—a process that always requires steering a course between extremes. The more we seek to replace historically specific concepts with more general terms—such as, by substituting "power" for "disciplinary power"—the more we risk losing the situational specificity which gives a Foucauldian version of the categorical imperative its genealogical rigor. On the other hand, the more narrowly we construe the categorical imperative, the more parochial will be the strategy it recommends.

At issue in the question of how broadly or narrowly to cast the categorical imperative is not a choice between the historical and the ahistorical. This distinction is ultimately untenable. Put otherwise, there is a limit to the degree to which a transcendental formula *can* move beyond the genealogical, for there simply are no pure concepts. Even Kant's various formulae of the categorical imperative require genealogical mediation, although he fails to notice this. For instance, the concepts of autonomy, legislation, the kingdom of ends, and so on are all genealogically derivative concepts with "birth certificates" which Kant fails to recognize. The same lesson must be applied to a Foucauldian ethics. We have neither a notion nor an experience of pure power—nor of disciplinary power—just as we have neither a notion nor an experience of ourselves as pure bodies.

Chapter Seven

"The Name of Lampe Must Now Be Entirely Forgotten": Kant in an Imaginary Voice

Critics of Kantian ethics argue not just against their formalism but also against the excessive denigration of desire and emotion as legitimate bases for ethical decision-making. Feminist critics in particular object that a rationalistic model of moral decision-making is a reflection of "masculine" experience rather than "feminine" experience—whether these categories are viewed from an essentialist or an antiessentialist perspective. Carol Gilligan's famous study claims that men are more likely to approach moral problems from a type of disconnected perspective, and that women are more likely to approach the same problems from an experience of connection.[1] Thus, men are more likely to think that emotional attachment is irrelevant to moral decision-making, while women tend to think that emotional attachment is an important factor.

The recent debate in analytic ethics over *impartiality* hinges on the related question of whether or not it is wrong to take into account our preferences when we are trying to figure out what the right thing to do would be in a particular situation.[2] Those who argue that we are at least entitled—or, on the strong view, obliged, in certain cases—to take into account our emotional connections to others fault Kant for his rejection of such appeals.[3] Once again, it is the rationalistic character of Kant's moral theory that is singled out for criticism.[4]

There are two distinct senses in which Kant's ethical theory might be called "rationalistic," and it is important to notice the difference between them. On the one hand, Kant's theory is rationalistic in that the categorical imperative bids us to act solely on the basis of rational considerations. This is the aspect of Kant's rationalism that his critics typically reject. However, the theory is also rationalistic in a different sense—namely, insofar as Kant claims to derive the categorical imperative solely from a consideration of the faculty of reason. This latter sense in which the theory is rationalistic would not, by itself, suffice to make it rationalistic in the former sense. After all, there is nothing contradictory in the idea of an ethical precept that would be derived from reason but would recommend that we act on our desires. For the same reason, the mere fact that the categorical imperative can be construed as a rationalistic principle does not *by itself* entail that it obliges us to reject all extrarationalistic considerations out of hand.

Addressing feminist critics of Kantian ethics, Seyla Benhabib introduces a useful distinction between "ethical cognitivism" and "ethical rationalism".

> By "ethical cognitivism," I understand the view that ethical judgments and principles have a cognitively articulable kernel, that they are neither mere statements of preference nor mere statements of taste. . . . By "ethical rationalism," by contrast, I mean a theoretical position which views *moral judgments* as the core of moral theory, and which neglects that the moral self is not a moral geometer, but an embodied, finite, suffering, and emotive being.[5]

Benhabib's point is that we can accept Kant's ethical cognitivism without having to accept his ethical rationalism as well. To be sure, even Benhabib's ethical cognitivism still involves an appeal to a type of court of reason before which we must submit the "validity claims" of our "principles." However, her basic point is that impartiality of a certain sort is compatible with an openness to a wide variety of historical factors that would include the preferences of persons.

A strictly impartial ethics would not be able to take sufficient account of relevant historical circumstances that would include things such as preferences. In cases of conflicting obligations, especially, preferences are of obvious moral and political relevance. Certainly freedom from disciplinary matrices cannot be attained by forbidding bodies from ever acting on their desires—as the case of Kant's failed care of the self should make all too clear.

At the heart of Kant's ethical rationalism is his view that the problem of freedom is the problem of how to act independently of all natural influence. However, once we recast the problem of freedom as the problem of how to get out of disciplinary matrices, the problem of heteronomously determined desires should be irrelevant. To be free from domination, one does not need to be completely free from heteronomous influence.

On the other hand, unless we assume the type of romantic view of Eros which Marcuse develops in *Eros and Civilization*, the problem of how to critique our desires is a real one.[6] To go back to the case of the prisoner's dilemma, suppose we imagine that one of the prisoners is suffering from Stockholm Syndrome—that is, the prisoner has developed an emotional attachment to someone who is trying to exercise a technique of mutual betrayal on her. In a case of this sort, the categorical imperative would be a useful reminder of what it would be like to take a more impartial view of what to do. To view the advice of an impartial perspective as irrelevant would be to advocate a type of dogmatic hedonism which fails to question the relationship between desire and power. Foucault's *History of Sexuality* shows that the ability to act on one's desires is not necessarily a sign of liberation.[7] While a Foucauldian categorical imperative obviously would not deem desire to be an impermissible basis for ethical decision-making, it would encourage us to question the political stakes of our desires. An example of this approach can be found in Sandra Bartky's critical reflection on the debate between what we might call the "hedonistic" defense of sadomasochism and the "monkish" castigation of it.[8]

Some of Kant's defenders have tried to ameliorate the strict impartiality of his moral theory by pointing out that autonomous inclinations could serve as a legitimate motive for Kant.[9] However, such a corrective would be too limiting, for it would continue to rule out the moral relevance of heteronomous desires. The problem of heteronomous desires is not that they are heteronomous, per se, but rather that they may be *bad* heteronomous desires. By retaining the categorical imperative as a general transcendental strategy, we are encouraged to consider whether our emotional attachments are leading us toward betrayal more effectively than would a more impartial attitude. However, this is just to say that the categorical imperative can be used to help us distinguish between desires that are good and desires that are bad. It is not to say that acting from desire is necessarily wrong.

If we look at the categorical imperative as a transcendental strategy which we arrive at by way of reflective judgment, then we can affirm both its recommended impartiality and its recognition of the relevance of preferences to maxim formation. The categorical imperative is retained as an impartial statement about how to resist techniques of mutual betrayal, while allowing for a thoroughly empirical strategizing with no reason to deem emotional considerations impermissible or irrelevant.

Kant's denigration of desires and emotions is connected more generally to his view that the transcendental cannot be mediated by the empirical. In her essay "Paradox A Priori" Luce Irigaray shows how, in the first *Critique*, the architectonic of reason functions as a transcendental home which man tries to build for himself without the help of nature. As rational architect, man thinks he is his own creator. For man to deny nature here is equivalent to man's denying that he is born of woman. Of course, sensuous nature plays a role in initiating the process whereby man comes to create himself. Just as man's empirical body must be born of woman, so experience must in some way inaugurate the construction of the architectonic of reason. However, the role that nature plays in this process is, for Kant, something that must be forgotten for man to retain his pretension to being an autonomous self-creator. Irigaray writes:

To build this construction, man was, of course, obliged to draw on reserves still in the realm of nature; a detour through the outer world was of course indispensable; the "I" had to relate to "things" before it could be conscious of itself. But this initial period of cooperative creation is forgotten in an arrogant claim to sovereign discretion over everything.[10]

Nature is supposed to provide a merely incidental occasion for the awakening of reason. Although the natural stimulus is prior in time, reason is still said to be logically "prior" to any encounter with nature, because the ground for the building which the culture of reason will construct must precede experience as its basis. Thus, even if the actual building comes after experience, its foundation is secured a priori. All empirical encounters with nature are mediated by this a priori foundation that makes nature's contribution all but irrelevant. Irigaray sees in this denial of nature, a denial of the mother. "The immediacy of *the relationship to the mother* is sacrificed."[11]

But "the pain of separation still stings." And the son resents this pain, not wanting to acknowledge that he is born of woman—not wanting to admit that the role of nature cannot be entirely repressed. On Irigaray's reading, the Kant/Sade and Kant/Masoch connections that we saw drawn by Lacan and Deleuze are related to this dialectic of inflicting/ suffering pain which son-subject experiences vis-a-vis mother-nature:

> Shall we place Kant next to Sade? Or, if the subtlety of his mind is given one quarter turn of the screw more—in or out—next to Masoch? . . . both to-gether, or neither simply one nor the other. The lawgiver is the cruel instrument implementing the rule, of course, but he is also forced into a painful respect for Nature (some of whose laws escape him), into suspending his feelings in the sight of beauty, and even into resenting that the pain of separation still stings.[12]

We can find further confirmation of Irigaray's reading by looking to Kant's care of the self once again. In chapter four, we saw the telos of Kant's regimen appear at night when he wrapped himself up like a cocoon. A cocoon, of course, is a type of egg outside the body of a mother, from which a living thing can hatch itself in a way that might seem autonomous. Kant, we know, emerged from his cocoon every morning at exactly 4:55. Curiously, it was at this very time of day that Kant's mother, Regina Dorothea Kant,[13] gave birth to her son Immanuel on 22 April 1724. Every morning, Kant's awakening would thereby attempt to turn a heteronomous birthing into an autonomous birthing.

But nature cannot be repressed entirely, and Kant may need assistance at his supposedly autonomous birthing. To maintain the illusion of masculine independence, though, it would be best to be assisted by a man, or rather, by a "man's man," a paragon of masculinity—say, by a former soldier or a bachelor. Someone, in short, like Martin Lampe. It is Lampe, Kant's manservant, who plays the role of midwife—or perhaps we should say "midhusband"— in Kant's daily birthing. He enters his master's bedchamber at exactly 4:55 every morning and announces that the time for labor has arrived. Having provided this occasion, Lampe withdraws immediately to boil hot water—for Kant's tea. (Perhaps he fetches clean towels as well.) Lampe provides the natural impetus for Kant to awaken from his critical slumbers much as another bachelor, David Hume, provides an occasion for Kant to awaken from his dogmatic slumbers.

When company is over for dinner, Kant likes to have Lampe inform the guests that he never once had to awaken his master a second time. One can imagine Kant's pleasure on such occasions—his self-discipline and his self-construction are shown to be autonomous by the fact that he needs only a single natural occasion to initiate the process.

A bit like Robert Bly, Kant sees Lampe and himself as brethren in the high order of bachelorhood. When Lampe announced one day that he was to renounce this order and marry a woman, Kant felt a deep sense of betrayal. "[Lampe's marriage] was the first cause of his dissatisfaction with his old servant."[14]

As a type of symbol of masculinity, Lampe also represents patriarchal discipline. From the Prussian army he learned that mechanical regularity which enabled him to assist Kant in his disciplinary regimen. However, while Kant admires Lampe's discipline, he bemoans the fact that Lampe entirely lacks culture. He complains that Lampe is "exceedingly ignorant," that he is incapable of writing, that he can never remember the name of the newspaper he daily fetches for Kant, and that he drinks excessive quantities of beer. Early on, Kant concludes that Lampe could learn only through severe discipline.

> His master was liberal towards him at first, but this encouraged him in his intemperate habits. . . . Kant became very suspicious of Lampe, and regarding severity as the only successful method of dealing with him, he treated him quite harshly.[15]

Man, according to Kant, requires more disciplining than does woman.[16] It should, therefore, be no surprise that Lampe—the very figure of masculinity—needs a good deal of it. But what especially troubles Kant is that Lampe seems incapable of rising above this need. Discipline should be but a first step in an educational process which is supposed to culminate in instruction through culture. Lampe seems stuck at the disciplinary stage—something that would not happen to a woman.

Being "more artistic, finer, and more regular" than man, "woman requires much less training and education, also less instruction, than man."[17] Woman is more naturally self-disciplined and, therefore, better prepared for moral culture than is man. For this reason, Rousseau is credited with "the important opinion" that "the cultivation by education of the character of girls would have the greatest influence on the male sex and upon morals generally."[18]

However, according to Kant, the type of education that a man needs is different from the sort that a woman needs. The souls of women—"the fair sex"—aspire to the "character of the beautiful," while the souls of men—"the noble sex"—

tend, rather, toward the sublime.[19] There is a clear difference between the sexes, which tells us that men and women must be educated differently. Conversely, the aim of this difference in education is to preserve the difference between the sexes—or more exactly, to maintain our ability to discern a difference.

> This must all education and instruction, and all endeavours to forward the moral perfection of both, have in view; unless the charming distinction, which nature intended to make between two human sexes, *shall be rendered indiscernible.*[20]

Kant's chief concern seems to be epistemological rather than ontological. How would we be able to tell the difference between the sexes if women received the same education as men? He couches this problem as an aesthetic one. "[Women] should fill their heads neither with battles from history, nor with forts from geography; *for it becomes them as little to smell of gunpowder, as men of musk.*"[21] However, it is clear that Kant is more concerned with a moral problem than he is with an aesthetic one. Anything that interferes with our ability to distinguish between the sexes is morally wrong. It is on this basis, for instance, that Kant condemns homosexuality. He calls it "contrary to the ends of humanity," and cites it as one example of several "*crimina carnis contra naturam,*" all of which "degrade human nature to a level below that of animal nature and make man unworthy of his humanity."[22] In Kant's view, men do not act like men when they engage in homosexual activity. They thereby blur the distinction between the sexes, which appears to be their chief "crime against nature."

Would anything that threatened to obscure the differences between the sexes be immoral for Kant? For instance, would it be immoral for a man to wear musk or for a woman to smell like gunpowder? What would happen if we could no longer tell the difference between men and women on the basis of smell—as might happen, say, if men were to cease to be associated with the smell of gunpowder?

As a matter of fact, Kant himself envisions just such a scenario—and not as a moral calamity, but, on the contrary, as a moral ideal. According to Kant, a prerequisite for perpetual peace—and the perfecting of the human race—is that "'Standing armies (*miles perpetuus*) will gradually be abolished altogether.' For they constantly threaten other states with war by the very fact that they are always prepared for it."[23] Kant views not just the end of warfare, but also the elimination of armies, as an essential condition for the perfection of humanity. In this latter respect, he differed from some other contemporary utopian theorists. For instance, five years after the publication of "Perpetual Peace," the Prussian military theorist A. H. D. von Bülow published his "Spirit of the Modern System of War," in which he claimed to have discovered mathematical principles for determining before the actual fighting which of two sides would win any given battle. All one needed to do, von Bülow argued, was calculate the forces and positions of the troops and the outcome could be determined, as it were, a priori. Inspired by Kant, von Bülow further predicted that his discovery had made it possible to realize a perpetual peace. It would simply be necessary to restructure the European map in such a way as to guarantee that any military endeavors would end in stalemate.[24]

Von Bülow's peace requires as its condition the continued maintenance of standing armies, whereas Kant's peace requires the abolition of armies. We can characterize the difference in their perspectives by noting that von Bülow outlines a MAD solution to the prisoner's dilemma construed as a game-theoretic problem, while Kant gives us an ethical solution to the dilemma construed as a disciplinary matrix problem. We can also contrast them by noting that von Bülow articulates a perpetual peace which allows men to smell like men—because they will continue to be associated with the smell of gunpowder—whereas in Kant's picture, men will only become fully human when they will have ceased to be associated with the smell of gunpowder. In other words, men will have to stop smelling like men in order to become fully human.

What will happen to the distinction between the sexes when men attain their full humanity—that is, when their smell will no longer be discernible from that of women? Moreover, because men will only become fully human when they give up the smell of gunpowder, does this mean that men who smell like men today are not yet real men? Or will men cease to be real men when they become fully human?

As a former Prussian officer, Lampe certainly carries with him the smell of gunpowder. Lampe also seems extremely recalcitrant to moral improvement. Could there be a connection here? If so, what is it?

Lampe, we know, can never seem to rise above his need for discipline. However, this means that Lampe—the figure of masculinity—can never seem to become fully human, for discipline is that which "changes animal nature into human nature."[25] Now, if women naturally need less discipline than men is it simply because women are less capable of rising above their animal nature? Or could it be that women are more naturally raised above the level of animal nature than men? Women, after all, are not associated with the smell of gunpowder. Who represents humanity here, and who is the "other" of humanity?

Kant confesses that he is unable to understand the nature of woman. For this reason, he cannot say what sort of difference there should be in the education of the sexes. In particular, he says that men understand nothing of what constitutes a feminine discipline. "Until we shall have studied feminine nature better, it is best to leave the education of daughters to their mothers, and to let them off from books . . . . each must discipline his own sex."[26] The same view is expressed in *Anthropology from a Pragmatic Point of View*. "Woman must train and discipline herself in practical matters: man understands nothing of this."[27]

One day, Kant suddenly dismissed Lampe from service, announcing that Lampe had done something unspeakable. "It was suspected that he had made an assault on Kant, who would never tell what he had done, but said, 'Lampe has so acted towards me that I am ashamed to state what he did.'"[28] Did Lampe make some sort of explicit sexual advance on Kant? Or did Kant suddenly become uncertain about the meaning of his relationship with his manservant? What exactly was Lampe's role in Kant's supposedly autonomous birthing all those years? Did he not provide the natural occasion for this process, planting the seed as it were? Did he not regularly enter Kant's bedchamber and ejaculate—"It is time!"—in order to initiate the process? Was Lampe merely a male "midhusband," or was he more? Kant's lover? Husband? Father?

On a scrap of paper Kant writes, "The name of Lampe must now be entirely forgotten."[29]

The imperative to forget the name of Lampe can be read in the light of Kant's moral condemnation of homosexuality. A man who approaches another man sexually "no longer deserves to be a person."[30] If Lampe did approach Kant sexually, Kant would have a moral obligation to stop thinking of Lampe as a human being. After all, Lampe would have committed the terrible crime of upsetting the natural division between the sexes.

But is it not Kant himself who, in calling for men to give up their unique smell, threatens to overthrow this natural division? Could we not read the imperative to forget the name of Lampe as an Imaginary demand to banish masculinity— the irreducible "other" of humanity symbolized by the perpetual smell of gunpowder? If Kant's reaction is homo- phobic, his is an ambiguous homophobia. On the one hand, there is the Symbolic homophobia which finds the masculine order threatened by any attempt to blur the distinction between the sexes. Yet, on the other hand, there is a type of Imaginary homophobia which is not a fear of homosexuality, but rather a fear of the masculine as such: *homophobia* in a more literal sense, expressing the "natural" demand that man be overcome. Nature, after all, could never be repressed entirely. Kant's care of the self could not prevent his body from experiencing becomings, just as his birth could not have taken place without the assistance of his mother. To be sure, all of this remains submerged in an Imaginary order, the depths of which Kant could never plumb. In Irigaray's words, "For the most sophisticated faculty of the senses, the imaginary, will remain the slave of the understanding."[31]

The need to record the banishment of the name of Lampe from his thoughts highlights the performative impossibility of carrying out this "must." Kant writes himself a note so that he will see the name of Lampe and *remember* it as the name that must be *forgotten*. He is condemned to perform the Sisyphean feat of remembering the name of Lampe in order to forget it. "I must forget the name of Lampe, I must not forget the name of Lampe"—a perpetual game of *fort/da*. Moreover, the dialectical structure of this double-bind makes it a type of becoming which Kant must reduce to an instantaneous accomplishment. "The name of Lampe must *now* be entirely forgotten" is an imperative whose demand must be met "on the spot."

Keeping to an Imaginary reading, we can read this imperative as saying that moral perfection is possible for man to achieve only if masculinity is remembered as something that must be forgotten. The *ought* here does not—cannot—imply *can*. The forgetting of the father, the transcending of a masculine discipline, the becoming-feminine of man—which, alone, is the becoming-human of man—all this is impossible. The name of Lampe functions as a transcendental limit prohibiting the necessary transgression of that name.

Read as a specific formulation of the categorical imperative—which, according to Kant, impels us to transcend the smell of gunpowder—who is speaking here? "The voice of the Father—or of the proscribed mother?"[32] Of his biological father, it is said that Kant "rarely referred to him," although he doubtless never forgot the strict discipline he suffered at his hands.[33] Kant's mother taught her children in a different way. "The character of Immanuel's mother was more positive than that of the father; and ... she made on him the deepest and most lasting impression."[34] Kant was to say that "her instruction has had an abiding and blessed influence on my life."[35] But what was the type of feminine discipline which she taught?

While the name of the father cannot be forgotten—or rather, must be retained in memory as something (not) to be forgotten—the name of the (forgotten) mother must not be forgotten. "Never shall I forget my mother, for she planted and nourished in me the first good seed."[36] The seed planted not by the father, nor by Lampe, but by Dorothea Regina, the mother whose example taught a type of discipline which Kant, because he was a man, was unable to comprehend. This is the seed that Kant would spend the rest of his life trying to birth himself. "If only I had been a girl when I learned my mother's discipline," he seems to say later, recognizing his failure but unable to do anything about it. For the return of the repressed Imaginary in Kant never rises to the surface—the power of the imagination is "an art concealed in the depths of the human soul, whose real modes of activity nature is hardly likely ever to allow us to discover, and to have open to our gaze."[37]

As Irigaray suggests, Kant's failure stems from his desire for pure transcendental principles. The denial of the mother and the denial of nature are equivalent to a denial of the genealogical.

In casting the categorical imperative juridically, Kant was obeying the Symbolic Law of the Father from the very first. However, if we approach the categorical imperative genealogically, we arrive, not at a principle of patriarchal domination, but, instead, at a genealogical call to resist its disciplinary matrices. Instead of giving up the transcendental impulse, we must situate it. Only then can we develop a critical questioning of the conditions of domination, speaking Kantian ethics in an Imaginary, genealogical voice.

Chapter Eight

Practicing Philosophy As a Discipline of Resistance

The transformation of the medieval *faculties* into academic *disciplines* is contemporaneous with the emergence of disciplinary power, and Kant's "The Conflict of the Faculties" straddles this period of transformation. How did the faculties become disciplines, and what does it mean to speak, today, of an academic "discipline"? What is the relationship between the discipline of philosophy and the other academic disciplines? What sort of discipline does the "discipline" of philosophy practice today? Is it a discipline of domination or a discipline of resistance? All of these questions, for several reasons, have a direct bearing on how we think through the Kantian legacy. First, there rages today a debate about the fate of philosophy as a discipline. Second, a metadeductive inquiry into the juridical model of critique must question the way in which this model has historically functioned within the discipline of philosophy. Third, because Kant himself played a crucial role in the development of philosophy *as* a discipline.

Because the academic disciplines are disciplinary in several entangled senses, it is important to understand the relationship among these different senses. In academia, a *discipline* is defined by its methodological rigor and the clear boundaries of its field of inquiry. Methods or fields are criticized as being "fuzzy" when they are suspected of lacking a discipline. In a more straightforwardly Foucauldian sense, the disciplinary power of academic disciplines can be located in their methods for producing docile bodies of different sorts. Within academic institutions proper, many such

116

practices come readily to mind. Students and faculty are regularly submitted to an immense variety of examinations, an obvious function of which is to produce subjects who are themselves advocates of the rules of the disciplines in question. Those who are said to have mastered a discipline are those who have been mastered by it. Hence, it is not surprising that, as Thomas Kuhn observes, disciplinary revolutions are more likely to be instigated by those who have not been trained by the discipline the rules of which they overthrow.[1] Outside the ivory tower, academic disciplines also function as the producers and distributors of generalizable techniques of disciplinary power. They furnish a wide variety of panoptical apparatuses with an array of techniques for the surveillance and manipulation of bodies. Virtually all of the examples of disciplinary practices which Foucault discusses in *Discipline and Punish* are either produced, refined, theorized, or, in some other way, mediated by some sort of academic discipline.

Despite the pivotal position of the academic disciplines in the various histories he reconstructs, Foucault never really focuses his attention on a genealogy of academic institutions as such. Of more concern to him than universities as specific sites of disciplinary power are schools for children, and these are not granted any privileged place. No differently from the hospital or the military camp, "The school became a sort of apparatus of uninterrupted examination."[2] As with hospital buildings and prison architecture, "the school building was to be a mechanism for training . . . . the very building of the École was to be an apparatus for observation."[3] The sites of disciplinary training are multiple and, for Foucault, do not involve a training of rationality so much as a molding of behavior. If any specific type of institution serves as an exemplary site of disciplinary techniques, it is not the school but the military camp. Foucault calls attention to "a military dream of society" that competed with the social compact models of the classical age.

> Historians of ideas usually attribute the dream of
> a perfect society to the philosophers and jurists of

the eighteenth century; but there was also a military dream of society. . . . While jurists or philosophers were seeking in the pact a primal model for the construction or reconstruction of the social body, the soldiers and with them the technicians of discipline were elaborating procedures for the individual and collective coercion of bodies.[4]

While Foucault is right to say that the military camp served as a paradigm for the organization of bodies, his strict dichotomy between philosophers and jurists on the one side, and the military utopian theorists on the other, is something of an oversimplification. For one thing, military theory became a type of philosophical discipline of its own at this time, and its practitioners explicitly drew on the works of those whom they saw as their fellow *Aufklärer*. We have seen, for instance, how von Bülow developed his militaristic utopian vision from his reading of Kant. What was unique about the emerging academic disciplines—including military theory—was their development of techniques for training bodies to think in desired ways, the classic examples of which became the techniques of mutual betrayal. We might generically refer to their "techniques of rationality." In the context of the militaristic model, these techniques consisted of ways of training bodies to freely deliberate and rationally choose to give up their freedom. The fierce loyalty of the Napoleonic soldiers until the bitter end of their devastating defeat in Russia can only be understood in the light of the sense of liberty which Napoleon could foster in the minds of the bodies he manipulated. By opposing the military dream of society to the philosophers' and jurists' shared dream of society, Foucault seems to treat disciplinary techniques of domination as not requiring a training of the rationality of bodies. He thereby overlooks the ways in which the emerging academic disciplines served to transform military training from a training of bodies-without-minds to a training of bodies-with-minds-of-a-certain-sort.

At least until the *History of Sexuality*, what seems to be missing from Foucault's work is a sense of the importance of the techniques of rationality, and of the central role that the academic disciplines have played in forging them as tools that could be dispersed throughout society. To be sure, Foucault highlights the importance of the emerging disciplines of economics, biology, and linguistics in *The Order of Things* as well as of psychology and medicine in almost all of his works. Nonetheless, when Foucault focuses on these disciplines, he examines, not how they train bodies to reason, but rather how they construct forms of rationality that are used as instruments for training bodies. The difference is important because, on Foucault's reading, the need to train *bodies* to reason in certain ways is less important than the need to train *those who exercise disciplinary control* over bodies to reason in certain ways. The academic disciplines have played both functions, not just the latter.

There are two reasons why Foucault tended not to notice the phenomena whereby techniques of rationality are directly exercised on bodies. The first has to do with his rejection of the paradigm of intellectual history, which treats academic disciplines as having pure epistemic stories that can be told without looking at issues concerning power. The second is that, unlike Marxist critics of intellectual history, Foucault also rejected an ideological model for telling the story of the academic disciplines.

In his critique of intellectual history, Foucault warns against treating the academic disciplines as if they were autonomous above-the-fray practices from which discoveries only happen to be applied in extra-academic settings afterwards. While not precluding the conceivability of a purely epistemic reconstruction of the possibility of a particular way of thinking—any more than he rules out a priori the possibility of transcendental philosophy—Foucault, nonetheless, rejects any methodology that would begin by separating the epistemic conditions for the possibility of a particular discipline's judgments from the historical conditions for the actuality of a discipline's bodies of statements. In the transition from intellectual history to archaeology and genealogy, what is given up is an assumption about the a priori possibility of demarcating the boundaries that distinguish the epistemic from the historical in any given field of power/knowledge. Intellectual history can only offer a dogmatic solution to this problem, one determined by the present's construal of what counts as the epistemic. Here, the shortcomings of intellectual history are the same as those of a pure transcendental philosophy.

However, Foucault's rejection of an ideological construal of power/knowledge formations is a different matter entirely. Unlike intellectual historians, theorists of ideology do not seek to rigidly separate the epistemic from the historic any more than does Foucault. On the other hand, ideological models of the disciplines tend to maintain some sort of separation between the substructural sphere of real power relations, and the superstructural sphere of ideological power relations. With his fusion of power/knowledge, Foucault seeks to show the untenability of any such distinction.

To be sure, there are models of false consciousness which are much more nuanced than a strict substructure/superstructure model would suggest. For this reason, some Marxist critics have wondered whether Foucault offered anything genuinely new with his notion of power/knowledge that had not already been thematized within the Marxist tradition—especially in critical theory.

Whether Foucault himself gives us the resources to explicate the distinction between power/knowledge and ideology is one which I will not discuss here, because I am more interested in thinking through the concept of power/knowledge—or, as I have suggested, power/judgment—from the standpoint of techniques of rationality. What is distinctive about the techniques of rationality is that they construct not just specific beliefs or even systems of belief, as ideology is supposed to do. Rather, they are forces designed to shape the very conditions for the possibility of experience. In other words, at issue in a struggle over techniques of rationality is nothing less than a struggle over the future history of the transcendental conditions for historical possibility.

Descriptions of how ideology is supposed to work tend to be based on the category of belief. An ideology is defined as a set of beliefs. Ideological mechanisms are described as ways of encouraging people to believe certain things. By contrast, a technique of rationality does not primarily aim at fostering specific beliefs—although, to be sure, this is a concomitant goal. More fundamentally, it seeks to foster ways of thinking which will be constitutive of the experience of the subjects which it trains to reason. The distinction might seem to be little more than a quibble—until, that is, we take seriously the idea that the transcendental has a history. Techniques of rationality do not merely form historically contingent systems of beliefs. They foster historically contingent conditions for the possibility of experience. At stake in a technique of rationality is an attempt to shape the transcendental.

To understand how history can produce the transcendental without thereby vitiating the transcendental character of the conditions for the possibility of historical experience itself, we must focus in much greater detail on the history of the schematizing role of power. A clue for how to think this through can be drawn from Horkheimer's and Adorno's *Dialectic of Enlightenment*. Drawing on the Kantian model of the schematism as the way in which concepts of the understanding are programmed to apply to appearances, Horkheimer and Adorno show how Hollywood films perform a training of rationality by showing their viewers how to schematize a pregiven set of concepts.[5] Building on this model—and expanding it to include, not only a set of merely empirical concepts and schemata, but whatever broader sets of concepts function as the conditions for the possibility of experience, we could tell the history of techniques of rationality as the inculcation of transcendental parameters of thought.

To some extent, this is precisely the sort of history which Hegel's *Phenomenology* seeks to explicate. However, Hegel focuses, not on deliberately exercised techniques of rationality, but rather on the ways in which human experience works up a historical transcendental behind-the-scenes, as it were. Indeed, when Hegel says that history is at an end, we can take him to be recognizing the emergence of the techniques of rationality. Spirit reaches its truth when it realizes that it can manipulate its limits—henceforth the history of the transcendental will not be blind. It will, rather, be a contested battlefield directed by disciplinary armies with specific transcendental agendas, so to speak, and each seeking to impart its own form of rationality. Thus, a continuation of Hegel's *Phenomenology* must begin from the active wielding of techniques which were once passively worked up from history. The posthistories of capitalism, communism, and fascism, for instance, could be told in this light. At stake in such movements is nothing less than the attempt to construct transcendental limits of the present.

However, here I wander far afield from the limits of this present project. The main point here is that we cannot ignore the peculiar role that the academic disciplines themselves play as schematizers of power in a disciplinary society. To attend to this distinctive role is not automatically to fall into the converse risk of exaggerating the role of intellectuals in history.

If one were to chart the apparently heterogeneous space of disciplinary formations, one would find a long ladder of metapanopticism at work. Just as everyday disciplinary apparatuses function panoptically, so do the academic disciplines seek to survey these instruments of surveillance. In the same way, so has the discipline of philosophy—since Kant, through Kant, and despite Kant—been traditionally the discipline which surveys the other disciplines. The metapanoptical role of the discipline of philosophy gives it a *potentially* important position in maintaining or undermining a vast network of disciplinary matrices. Kant not only saw this, but he himself helped to construct this metapanoptical structure in order to position philosophy as a discipline of resistance. He saw himself as protecting philosophy from the disciplinary control of the other faculties as well as the state which had the authority to control the "higher" faculties. However, Kant could no more rigorously distinguish between a discipline of resistance and a discipline of domination here than he could in his care of the self or in his moral philosophy. Hence, his was a Pyrrhic victory for the emergent discipline of philosophy, a detailed history of which would show how, since Kant, it has recapitulated the same aporias that bifurcate and unite a discipline of resistance with a discipline of domination in Kant.

On the face of it, "The Conflict of the Faculties" appears to be a series of "turf battles," in which Kant seeks to establish the right of the philosophy faculty to critique the claims of the other faculties. However, it is clear that Kant's larger battle pits philosophy against the state, for it is the state which controls the higher faculties and which, Kant argues, should not have the right to censor the faculty of philosophy. Kant wants to show that, while the state may be entitled to censor the "higher faculties"—theology, law, and medicine—it is not entitled to censor the lower faculty of philosophy. The higher faculties must teach doctrines that are sanctioned by the state and are, thus, legitimately subject to censorship. However, because philosophers seek the truth, they cannot be forced to teach a doctrine merely on authority.

> Now the power to judge autonomously—that is, freely (according to principles of thought in general)—is called reason. So the philosophy faculty, because it must answer for the truth of the teachings it is to adopt or even allow, must be conceived as free and subject only to laws given by reason, not by government.[6]

Kant's strategy is, in effect, to appeal to the legitimacy of the juridical model of philosophy. Just as the critical court of reason cannot be overruled by the dogmatic court of reason, it also cannot be overruled by any court of the state.[7]

Here, we see Kant coming closest to putting forth a metadeductive defense of the juridical model of critique—although he casts this metadeduction itself in terms that are still juridical. It is a question of establishing a right of jurisdiction. Who has the right to preside over the juridical questions that concern philosophy? In effect, Kant claims to deduce—in the juridical sense—the right of the court of reason in this case. He does not seek to argue against censorship per se, but rather to ask which court has the right to censor. For this reason, a *critique* of reason and a *censorship* of reason are not diametrically opposed terms. In the first *Critique*, Kant contrasts an illegitimate or dogmatic censorship of reason with a legitimate or critical censorship. "A procedure of this kind—subjecting the facts of reason to examination, and if necessary to blame—may be entitled the *censorship* of reason."[8]

Yet, at the same time, Kant contrasts censorship—the extirpating of particular errors—with the more wholesale corrective of critique proper. The critical court of reason must "subject to examination, not the facts of reason, but reason itself, in the whole extent of its powers." This, Kant insists, is not censorship at all, but genuine critique. "This is not the censorship but the *criticism* of reason."[9]

It is precisely here that the question of discipline arises. More thorough than a mere censoring of reason is the disciplining of reason which critique undertakes. "Particular errors can be got rid of by *censure*," Kant writes, but, in the case of critique, "a quite special negative legislation seems to be required, erecting a system of precautions and self-examination under the title of a *discipline*."[10] In practicing self-discipline, critique undertakes a thorough-going correction that is designed to preclude the very possibility of certain errors arising.[11]

Because it presides over the critical court of reason, the faculty of philosophy should be exempt from state censorship. However, Kant wants more than just to protect philosophy from state censorship. He wants to extend the jurisdiction of the critical court to cover some of the territory occupied by the higher faculties. "The philosophy faculty's function in relation to the three higher faculties is to control (*controlliren*) them and, in this way, be useful to them."[12] In calling for the right of the philosophy faculty to discipline the other faculties—*sie zu controlliren*—Kant claims the critical court's right to evaluate their claims. Here, he suggests that the faculty of philosophy and the state share a common interest, for example in objecting to the faculty of law's claim that the perfection of the state is impossible. Kant calls the theory about the intractable wickedness of man's nature a "terroristic manner of representing human history."[13]

If a doctrine is terroristic, should the philosophy faculty have the right to censor it? Does Kant seek to establish the critical court's right to censor the other faculties? On Jacques Derrida's reading, Kant resists this move because of the way in which he distinguishes the concepts of censorship and critique.

> The Kantian definition of censorship is simple: a *critique* which has force ("Gewalt") at its disposal. Pure force in itself does not *censor* and, furthermore, would not be able to have a bearing on discourses or texts in general. Neither is a critique without power able to censor.[14]

While Kant affirms the state's entitlement to censor the higher faculties, he does not ask that philosophy be granted the role of censor. The discipline of critique does not involve the same exercise of force which censorship demands. As Derrida observes:

> Since he always insists that the Faculty of Philosophy should not have any executive power at its disposal and should never be able to give orders, Kant must come to refuse it the *right* of censorship, which is inseparable from the power of censorship, even in concept.[15]

Derrida's argument might seem to blur the distinction between two types of censorship—state censorship and critical censorship. After all, critical censorship has the *force of reason* on its side. The discipline of philosophy may be a discipline without state power, but it has legitimate recourse to the power of reason. However, Derrida is right to note that the critical court of reason is not entitled to exercise the state's right to censor the other faculties. Critical censoring might thus be better dubbed a censuring.

Philosophy censures in the interest of truth, whereas the government censors in the interest of utility. Nonetheless, Kant suggests, the state might appreciate a certain utility in having the faculty of philosophy around to discipline the higher faculties. "For the government may find the freedom of the philosophy faculty, and the increased insight gained from this freedom, a better means for achieving its ends than its own absolute authority."[16] The philosophy faculty serves the state by practicing a type of discipline on itself and on the other faculties. In pointing out that philosophy's discipline might serve the state's ends, Kant is, doubtless, thinking of an ideal government rather than a corrupt one. In "Perpetual Peace," he argues that philosophers might help advise the rulers of republican governments as to how to reconcile the demands of politics with the demands of morality. No doubt, in "The Conflict of the Faculties" he conceives of the possible utility of philosophy in the same way. Nonetheless, Kant's notion of a court of reason that has the task of disciplining the other faculties is dangerously close to precisely what he tries to avoid. Once again, this danger arises because he has not thought through the metadeductive question concerning his juridical model of critique. Kant's attempt to vouchsafe autonomy for the faculty of philosophy exactly parallels the plan of his practical philosophy. One type of discipline will be pursued as a means for warding off another type. This practice exhibits the same type of ambiguity that we see in Kant's care of the self and in his moral theory— it fluctuates uncritically between practicing a genuine discipline of resistance and becoming an accomplice to a discipline of domination.

It is the critical court's status as a sort of metafaculty— or metadiscipline—which entitles it to be free from the jurisdiction of the state. In the post-Kantian Anglo-European world, the discipline of philosophy inherited not only Kant's juridical model, but also its "deduced" authority to judge the other disciplines. Just as Kant's critical court of reason was supposed to watch over and correct the judgments of the dogmatic court of reason, so the discipline of philosophy was, at least until recently, expected to play a metadisciplinary role in juridically reviewing the claims of the other academic disciplines.[17] In the nineteenth and early twentieth centuries this metadisciplinary role meant that philosophers were entitled to explain what it was that the other disciplines were doing and to tell them what they should be doing. This can be seen, not only in the obvious case of Hegel, but also in the logical positivists' claim to lay bare the foundations of the sciences, as well as in Heidegger's claim in *Being and Time* that it is philosophers who specify the appropriate ontology for all ontical spheres of investigation.

Both Habermas and Rorty have urged the disappearance of philosophy's metadisciplinary roles as usher and judge.[18] However, whether this is a good thing should depend on the degree to which the discipline of philosophy is—or can be turned into—a discipline of resistance as opposed to a discipline of domination. Before we agree or disagree with those who call for the "end of philosophy," we would need to undertake a detailed metadeduction of the juridical model of the discipline of philosophy today. Such an inquiry must consider carefully the two sorts of discipline that a discipline of philosophy can promise or peril. Moreover, we could not raise the metadeductive question in an ahistorical fashion, but must pose it genealogically, tracing the vicissitudes of the discipline since Kant. Obviously, such an undertaking is beyond the scope of this book.[19] Here, by way of a conclusion, I will outline what I take to be the political stakes involved in philosophy's recent death wish.

Today, we cannot accept Kant's assumption that a discipline of philosophy is automatically suited to be an instrument of resistance. Yet, we should be equally suspicious of the opposite one-sided perspective. There are two common assumptions that are frequently made by many of those who see themselves as furthering Foucauldian thinking.

The first is that the discipline of philosophy is politically irrelevant. This assumption, I think, tends to confuse something that has been depoliticized with something that is nonpolitical. What we need, as I have suggested, is a genealogical inquiry that would show how philosophy has inherited its depoliticized character. Such a study would enable us to think through the possibilities for revitalizing philosophy as a potentially effective discipline of resistance.

The second assumption is that all academic disciplines—
simply by virtue of being disciplines—are instruments of
domination. In America today, many academics working in
the disciplines of literature and philosophy seem to think
that, to attack the disciplinary as such—or what is sometimes
called the "disciplinarity" of the academic disciplines—is, in
every case, a radically emancipatory gesture. Any work that
crosses disciplinary boundaries is viewed a priori as some
type of revolutionary praxis.

Poststructuralism has been an important catalyst for this
academic ethos. For Roland Barthes, for instance, "breaking
down the walls" of the academic disciplines is about
equivalent to storming the Bastille.

> The *interdisciplinarity* which is today held up as a prime
> value in research cannot be accomplished by the
> simple confrontation of specialist branches of
> knowledge. Interdisciplinarity is not the calm of an
> easy security; it begins *effectively* (as opposed to the
> mere expression of a pious wish) when the solidarity
> of the old disciplines breaks down—perhaps even
> violently.[20]

Foucault also frequently characterized his own work as
operating in the "interstices" between the disciplines.
Operating outside the clearly demarcated disciplines was
one way of resisting the limits of the present.

While we can certainly agree with the poststructuralist
call for a radical questioning of disciplinary boundaries, we
should not assume that the disciplinary as such is something
that must be resisted in all its guises. For one thing, we
need to consider the degree to which the disciplinary
character of the disciplines can enable them to function as
sites of resistance. Moreover, we must ask the types of
genealogical questions that would lead us to understand
where the anti- or interdisciplinary impulse comes from in
the first place. Might it not be called forth by the disciplines
themselves—as, for instance, in the case of professional
philosophers calling for the end of their own discipline? The
interdisciplinary impulse can simply serve to turn microdis-
ciplines into macrodisciplines, without considering whether

this is linking up apparatuses of domination or of resistance. Conversely, the antidisciplinary impulse can arise just when a discipline is on the verge of transforming itself from a discipline of domination into a discipline of resistance. The theory of communicative action has yet to be questioned on precisely these same grounds. The linking up of separate spheres of rationality into a type of metarational public court is fraught with disciplinary ambiguity. (However, this is also a question for another project.)

Kant's ideal of a metadisciplinary questioning in effect promises to distinguish disciplines of domination from disciplines of resistance. However, Kant failed to ask the types of genealogical questions that would have enabled him to undertake a metadeduction of the juridical model of his metadiscipline. "The Conflict of the Faculties" remains a pivotal and extremely ambiguous text for these two reasons.

Derrida highlights the ambiguity of Kant's position by pointing out the strengths and weaknesses of Schelling's antidisciplinary critique of it. On Schelling's reading, Derrida notes, there are "two Kants".

> There is the Kant . . . who wants a department of philosophy to exist and to be protected (in particular from the state). . . . And then there is the Kant who grants the Faculty of Philosophy the right of critical and panoptical supervision over all the other departments.[21]

Schelling objects to Kant's willingness to allow the higher faculties—theology, law, and medicine—to be "tied to the power of the state they represent," while exempting "philosophy, over which the ruling power has no right of censure."[22] He notes that "in the Kantian apparatus, the Faculty of Philosophy remains determined and limited by the power of the state."[23] Thus, in Derrida's words, Schelling "insinuates that Kant subjects the department of philosophy, in a public institution, to the external power of the state; and that in this he does not understand the practice and place of philosophy in society in a liberal enough way."[24]

Instead of a type of covert "statism" which results from Kant's attempt to protect the integrity of the discipline of philosophy, Schelling recommends dismantling the discipline, arguing that there should be no separate philosophy faculty at all. In this way, a freer philosophy will flourish among all the members of a genuinely liberal society. (This, of course, is strikingly similar to Rorty's ideal.) As Kant seeks protection from the state through the integrity of a discipline, Schelling seeks such protection in the disintegration of this discipline.

Derrida agrees with Schelling's diagnosis of the risk involved with Kant's disciplinary construal of philosophy. However, he finds that a comparable risk arises with Schelling's desire to eliminate the discipline of philosophy altogether. By "breaking down the wall" (to use Barthes's phrase) which separates the lower faculty from the higher faculties, Schelling is willing to give up the integrity of a specific site for questioning the state. Without any disciplinary boundaries, we would have a public space that merges with the state. In his wholesale antidisciplinary stance, Schelling thereby risks a type of "totalizing absolutization of the state that Kant in his turn would have deemed dangerous and not very liberal."[25] Derrida calls attention to the "paradoxical logic" according to which "the hyperliberalism set over against Kant always carries the risk of turning into the temptation of totalization; . . . its consequences can reverse the liberal requirements."[26] Any hasty decision to undermine the academic disciplines runs the risk of merely reinscribing the panoptical functioning of the state or of other apparatuses of disciplinary domination.[27]

For these reasons, Derrida suggests, it might be better to strengthen the integrity of something like a discipline of philosophy. He and others have worked toward this end with the institution of the Collège International de Philosophie.[28] As a type of discipline of philosophy which seeks to question *the* discipline of philosophy, so to speak, the Collège puts itself forward as something like a metadeductive discipline of resistance.[29] Its aim is not to indiscriminately attack the disciplinary aspects of philosophy. Rather, it seeks "a new sort of relationship between philosophy and other fields, other disciplines. Constituted disciplines or disciplines to be constituted—new disciplines."[30] Derrida adds.

> We have nothing against interdisciplinarity: it is a very necessary thing which makes for progress in *some* institutions: but not enough. . . . What we want to do is not simply inter-disciplinarity, which implies that we have already identified objects and competences—that we know what these objects are.[31]

Derrida advocates the multiplication of disciplines. Instead of positioning any single discipline of philosophy in a unique metadisciplinary position, this would open up the university structure to allow for what we might call a "free play of faculties."[32]

In Kant's day, the state constructed the primary disciplinary matrices from which he sought to free the discipline of philosophy. Today, the integrity of philosophy as a discipline of resistance cannot be secured simply by keeping the state out of the university because our universities are themselves disciplinary matrices in a way that they were only beginning to be when Kant wrote his essay. As Derrida notes, the simple opposition between the university and the state can no longer be maintained.[33]

The difficulty with challenging any disciplinary matrix manifests itself in the difficulty of extricating philosophy from its juridical model. To put the discipline on trial, of course, would be to "lose the case" by performative contradiction. On the other hand, to attempt a nonjuridical critique of philosophy poses its own set of problems, the difficulty of which can be measured by the fact that, every time someone tries to undertake such a critique, the law-abiding philosophers invariably cry out, "That's not philosophy!" Hence, the later Wittgenstein is not a philosopher but a "mystic." Heidegger is not a philosopher but a "fuzzy thinker" or "some kind of poet." Derrida is "just a playful charlatan." The violence of such dismissals is usually in proportion to the seriousness of the attempted challenge to the discipline's juridical model.

This is not to say that Wittgenstein, Heidegger, Derrida, or anyone else has developed a thorough metadeduction of the discipline's juridical model, nor to deny that much of what passes for a challenge to the discipline deserves its charge of being unphilosophical. After all, there is—at times—something too mystical about Wittgenstein, too fuzzy (not to say arrogant) about Heidegger, and too playful in Derrida. This does not mean their work is bad philosophy. Rather, it simply shows how difficult it is to think outside the juridical model of philosophical rigor.

Also, for this reason, it is difficult to give an answer to the inevitable *ti esti* questions of the discipline of philosophy. A *ti esti* question is, of itself, essentially juridical, asking for a legal charge against some subject. Derrida has long resisted delineating either a method or proper subject matter for his deconstructions for just this reason. To define "deconstruction" would be to risk instituting the wrong sort of a single discipline of deconstruction. As was Foucault, Derrida has been frequently criticized for failing to issue definite judgments—especially ethical judgments. As with Foucault, I suspect, his reluctance to do so arises from a fear that one cannot *judge* without *passing judgment*—that is, that we cannot develop a nonjuridical ethic. However, if we reject a juridical model of judgment, then it should become possible to make specific judgments without passing judgment. Unlike a deconstruction—which seems to resist judgment altogether—a metadeduction must aim at providing the resources for a discipline of resistance. As such, it must formulate strategic judgments in a way that a deconstruction, perhaps, cannot.

In "The Discourse on Language," Foucault contrasts the disciplines with the sciences, and he takes the distinguishing mark to be the former's status as regimes which allow for a limited construction of new sorts of statements.

> We have to recognise another principle of limitation in what we call, not sciences, but "disciplines." Here is yet another relative, mobile principle, one which enables us to construct, but within a narrow framework.[34]

What can be constructed is circumscribed by the rules of a given discipline. "Within its own limits, every discipline recognises true and false propositions, but it repulses a whole teratology of learning."[35] It is not simply that a discipline can proclaim certain statements to be false, but that it can rule out as illegitimate certain types of statements which, from the discipline's perspective, would consequently be neither true nor false, but simply monstrous. All of the disciplines—not just the discipline of philosophy—define as monstrous any statement that operates outside of philosophy's juridical model.

That its juridical model is so crucial to the discipline of philosophy is evidenced by the hostility with which trained philosophers react to anyone who attempts to question it. Not surprisingly, this hostility manifests itself under the form of a trial of those would escape it. For instance, the "case against Heidegger," which has drawn so much attention recently, provides an interesting illustration of the degree to which the discipline of philosophy is today committed to its juridical model. For years, philosophy departments have resisted even acknowledging as philosophy any continental work that seems to depart from this model. Because Heidegger sought to think beyond the juridical model, he was considered to be an enemy within the discipline long before any professional philosopher paid any attention to his involvement with the Nazis. The sudden fervor to convict Heidegger is as much of an opportunistic attempt to preserve a certain notion of what philosophy should be, as it is a genuine expression of moral outrage at Heidegger, the person. In finding him guilty, the court of reason simply reaffirms its own legitimacy. (For that matter, even acquittal can perform a similar self-legitimating role, except that, in the case of Heidegger, that would be to preserve the possible legitimacy of a philosophy that tried to think beyond the juridical.)

The discipline saves its special wrath for those who resist the simple convict-or-acquit model of addressing philosophical accusations of any sort. When Derrida refuses to simply convict or acquit either Heidegger or his friend Paul

de Man, his disciplinary critics go for the jugular immediately. In the desire for a "verdict" against Derrida for not
issuing a verdict against Heidegger, we see how threatening
it is to the discipline to think in any terms other than the
juridical. We also see that at least one of the functions of
the discipline's juridical model is to control those who do
not conform to its rules. One need only think of most
professional American philosophers' attitudes toward those
who ask deconstructive and feminist questions to get a sense
of this will-to-dominate those who resist the rules of the
discipline.

To be sure, there are some contemporary philosophers
who are actively questioning whether philosophy "ought"
to be conducted in an *argumentative* way. Rorty, for instance,
defends his notion of an "edifying philosophy" with an
argument against argumentation.[36] But to challenge the
argumentative model is not necessarily the same as
questioning the juridical model of the discipline. Moreover,
even if we were to view them as equivalent, merely to
recommend that we abandon the agonistic model, would
be to leave *undeduced*—and hence, lurking—either the same
juridical model or the same form of power that it masks.
Finally, Rorty simply recommends eradicating the discipline
of philosophy instead of transforming it into a genuine
discipline of resistance. Rather perniciously, I think, he has
encouraged philosophers to laugh at the idea that we
might—as philosophers—play an important role in society.
(When Virginia Held recently called for philosophers to take
political stands *"as philosophers,"* her suggestion fell on deaf
ears.[37]) As it is practiced today, the discipline of philosophy
does appear to be politically irrelevant. However, this is the
result of a long process of the depoliticization of philosophy,
a process which began with Kant's ambiguous institution
of philosophy as a discipline.

Rightly or wrongly, Kant's contemporaries viewed the
French Revolution as having resulted, in large part, from
the work of the *philosophes*. They viewed themselves as
capable of making a difference, and "The Conflict of the
Faculties" is designed to preserve this capability. Since Kant,

however, the discipline has tended to function as an instrument of domination rather than as an instrument of resistance. Many of those philosophers who would seem to be exceptions to this rule—the Young Hegelians, Marx, Kierkegaard, Nietzsche, Sartre, Derrida, and Irigaray—were either excluded from the academy or else have been ridiculed by it. Where the discipline of philosophy has served the forces of domination, it has been able to survive. Fairly or unfairly, "Hegel in Berlin" serves as a figure for this, and "Russell in America" could as well. On the other hand, where philosophy has threatened to function as a discipline of resistance, it has withered. The banalization of analytic philosophy is an obvious case in point. The discipline has flourished to the degree that it has become irrelevant to the life-world. Whatever would seem to remain as the potential for a discipline of resistance has been regularly effaced. Hence, the frequent and avid calls—by philosophers—for the end of their discipline. Philosophers practice a discipline of domination whenever they seek to "cure" themselves of any metadisciplinary impulses that might threaten to interfere with the "comfortable, smooth, reasonable" functioning of the technical disciplines.[38]

Must this be philosophy's only possible future? Has the time to realize it, as Adorno suggested, really passed? Or can we, once again, attempt to practice philosophy as a genuine discipline of resistance?

Notes

Preface

1. David Couzens Hoy, "Introduction," in *Foucault: A Critical Reader*, ed. David Couzens Hoy, (New York: Blackwell, 1986) 8.

Chapter One

1. Immanuel Kant, *Critique of Pure Reason*, trans. Norman Kemp Smith (New York: St. Martin's, 1965) Axi–xii.

2. Ibid., Axi.

3. Ibid., A13/B27.

4. Ibid., Axxi.

5. Ibid., A14/B28.

6. Ibid., A87/B119.

7. Dieter Henrich, "Kant's Notion of a Deduction and the Methodological Background of the First *Critique*" in *Kant's Transcendental Deductions*, ed. Eckart Förster (Stanford, Calif.: Stanford University Press, 1989), 32.

8. Ibid., 34.

9. As Henrich notes, the legal practice of deduction writing upon which Kant modeled his critique was a dying practice in his day. With the collapse of the Holy Roman Empire and the advent of post-Napoleonic legal practices, the practice of deduction writing disappeared completely. "The practice of deductions reaches back to a time when the tradition of Roman law was not yet revitalized and the modern theory of law had not yet been founded." Ibid., 33.

10. Gillian Rose, *Dialectic of Nihilism: Post-Structuralism and Law* (New York: Basil Blackwell, 1984) 1.

11. Garbis Kortian, *Metacritique: The Philosophical Argument of Jürgen Habermas*, trans. John Raffan (New York: Cambridge University Press, 1980) 28–29.

12. Jürgen Habermas, *Knowledge and Human Interests*, trans. Jeremy J. Shapiro, (Boston: Beacon, 1971) 13.

13. Ibid.

14. Ibid., 30.

15. Ibid., 42.

16. Ibid., 42.

17. Jürgen Habermas, "Philosophy as Stand-In and Interpreter" in *After Philosophy: End or Transformation*, ed. Kenneth Baynes et al. (Cambridge. Mass.: The MIT Press, 1987) 296–297.

18. Ibid., 297.

19. Ibid., 298.

20. Ibid.

21. Ibid., 299.

22. Habermas, *Knowledge and Human Interests* 3.

23. Kortian, 119.

24. Kortian, 120. Italics added.

25. Richard J. Bernstein, "Foucault: Critique as a Philosophical Ethos" in *Philosophical Interventions in the Unfinished Project of Enlightenment*, ed. Axel Honneth et al. (Cambridge: The MIT Press, 1992) 290.

26. Quoted in Richard J. Bernstein, *The New Constellation* (Cambridge, Mass.: The MIT Press, 1992) 202.

27. Habermas, *Knowledge and Human Interests* 7.

28. Ibid., 21.

29. Richard Dien Winfield, *Overcoming Foundations: Studies in Systematic Philosophy* (New York: Columbia University Press, 1989) 31–32.

30. Here, I am drawing on John McCumber's forthcoming reading of Hegel's theory of language. John McCumber, *The Company of Words* (Evanston, Ill.: Northwestern University Press, 1993).

31. Reiner Schürmann, *Heidegger on Being and Acting: From Principles to Anarchy*, trans. Christine-Marie Gros (Bloomington: Indiana University Press, 1987) 156. Italics added.

32. Ibid., 157.

33. John McCumber uses this term to characterize Hegel and Heidegger. John McCumber, *Poetic Interaction: Language, Freedom, Reason* (Chicago: The University of Chicago Press, 1989) 25.

Chapter Two

1. Michel Foucault, *Discipline and Punish: The Birth of the Prison*, trans. Alan Sheridan (New York: Vintage, 1979) 191–192.

2. Ibid., 183.

3. Ibid., 182.

4. Michel Foucault, *The History of Sexuality: Vol. 1: An Introduction*, trans. Robert Hurley (New York: Vintage, 1990) 86.

5. Ibid., 86.

6. Michel Foucault, *The Archaeology of Knowledge and the Discourse on Language*, trans. A. M. Sheridan Smith (New York: Pantheon Books, 1972) 86–87.

7. Ibid., 127.

8. Michel Foucault, "A Historian of Culture," in *Foucault Live: (Interviews, 1966–84)* (New York: Semiotext(e), 1989) 79.

9. Ibid., 79.

10. Michel Foucault, "What is Enlightenment?" in *The Foucault Reader*, ed. Paul Rabinow (New York: Pantheon, 1984) 34.

11. Ibid., 46.

12. McCumber, *Poetic Interaction: Language, Freedom, Reason* (Chicago: The University of Chicago Press) 17.

13. Foucault, "What is Enlightenment?" 43.

14. Ibid., 37.

15. Ibid., 45.

16. Ibid., 46.

17. Ibid., 46.

18. Nancy Fraser, *Unruly Practices: Power, Discourse, and Gender in Contemporary Social Theory* (Minneapolis: University of Minnesota Press, 1989) 56.

19. See, for instance, Michel Foucault, "Foucault Responds to Sartre" in *Foucault Live* 35–39.

20. Fraser, *Unruly Practices* 29.

21. Ibid., 30.

22. Jürgen Habermas, *The Philosophical Discourse of Modernity*, trans. Frederick Lawrence, (Cambridge, Mass.: The MIT Press, 1987) 274.

23. Ibid., 284–285.

24. Gillian Rose, *Dialectic of Nihilism:* Post-Structuralism and Law (New York: Basil Blackwell, 1984) 1.

25. Ibid., 171.

26. Ibid., 173–174.

27. Ibid., 207.

28. Michel Foucault, "Two Lectures" in *Power/Knowledge: Selected Interviews and Other Writings 1972–1977*, ed. Colin Gordon, trans. Colin Gordon et al. (New York: Pantheon, 1980) 96.

29. For one thing, both Foucault and Nietzsche are better read as continuing rather than abandoning the Kantian project of critique. For another, neither is best characterized as a nihilist.

30. See, for example, Rainer Rochlitz, "The Aesthetics of Existence: Post-Conventional Morality and the Theory of Power in Michel Foucault" in *Michel Foucault Philosopher*, trans. and ed. Timothy J. Armstrong (New York: Routledge, 1992) 248–258.

Chapter Three

1. "Many disciplinary methods had long been in existence—in monasteries, armies, workshops. But in the course of the seventeenth and eighteenth centuries the disciplines became general formulas of domination." Michael Foucault, *Discipline and Punish: The Birth of the Prison*, trans. Alan Sheridan (New York: Vintage, 1979) 137.

2. Ibid., 140. Discipline is "always meticulous, often minute. . . . Discipline is a political anatomy of detail." Ibid., 139.

3. "*Es hat vielleicht nie ein Mensch gelebt, der eine genauere Aufmerksamkeit auf seinen Körper und auf alles, was diesen betrifft, angewandt hat als Kant.*" Reinhold Bernhard Jachmann, "Immanuel Kant *geschildert in Briefen an einen Freund*" in *Wer War Kant?*, ed. Siegfried Drescher (Tübingen: Neske, 1974) 196.

4. Thomas De Quincey, "The Last Days of Immanuel Kant" in *The English Mail-Coach and Other Essays* (New York: Dutton, 1961) 177.

5. Ibid., 183.

6. Ibid., 175–176.

7. Foucault, *Discipline and Punish*, 23. Italics added.

8. Immanuel Kant, *Critique of Pure Reason*, trans. Norman Kemp Smith (New York: St. Martin's, 1965) Bxxv.

9. Ibid., A709/B737.

10. Ibid., A 711/B 739.

11. Ibid., A709–710/B737–738.

12. Ibid., A 711/B 739.

13. Foucault, *Discipline and Punish*, 184.

14. Kant, *Critique of Pure Reason*, A803/B831.

15. Gilles Deleuze, *Kant's Critical Philosophy: The Doctrine of the Faculties*, trans. Hugh Tomlinson and Barbara Habberjam, (Minneapolis: University of Minnesota Press, 1984) 27.

16. Immanuel Kant, *Education*, (Ann Arbor: University of Michigan Press, 1960) 1.

17. Ibid., 83.

18. Immanuel Kant, *The Metaphysics of Morals*, trans. Mary Gregor (New York: Cambridge University Press, 1991) 273.

19. Ibid., 273.

20. Foucault, *Discipline and Punish*, 180.

21. "The historical moment of the disciplines was the moment when an art of the human body was born. . . . What was then

being formed was a policy of coercions that act upon the body, a calculated manipulation of its elements, its gestures, its behaviour. . . . Thus discipline produces subjected and practised bodies, 'docile' bodies." Foucault, *Discipline and Punish*, 137–138.

22. This period coincides with the last years of Kant's life. "By the end of the eighteenth and the beginning of the nineteenth century, the gloomy festival of punishment was dying out." Foucault, *Discipline and Punish*, 8.

23. Kant, *The Metaphysics of Morals*, 273–274.

24. "If men knew what Good was, and knew how to conform to it, they would not need laws." Deleuze, *Kant's Critical Philosophy*, x.

25. "Kant reverses the relationship of the law and the Good. . . . It is the Good which depends on the law, and not vice versa." Ibid., x.

26. Ibid., x–xi.

27. *"Lorsque Kant parle au contraire de 'la' loi morale, le mot morale désigne seulement la détermination de ce qui reste absolument indéterminé: la loi morale est la représentation d'une pure forme, indépendante d'un contenu et d'un objet, d'un domaine et de circonstances. La loi morale signifie LA LOI, la forme de la loi, comme excluant tout principe supérieur capable de la fonder. En ce sens, Kant est un des premiers qui rompent avec l'image classique de la loi, et qui nous ouvrent une image proprement moderne."* Gilles Deleuze, *Présentation de Sacher-Masoch* (Paris: Les éditions de Minuit, 1967) 72.

28. *"Sade et Masoch représentent les deux grandes entreprises d'une contestation, d'un renversement radical de la loi."* Ibid., 75. "Deleuze presents Sade and Masoch as idealists, but idealists of a very peculiar kind. Sade's ideal is a delusion of pure reason, a primary nature of absolute negation. . . . Kant's moral imperative is ironically scorned in Sade's superior institutions of principled destruction." Ronald Bogue, *Deleuze and Guattari*, (New York: Routledge, 1989) 53–54.

29. Max Horkheimer and Theodor W. Adorno, *Dialectic of Enlightenment* (New York: Continuum, 1991) 95–96.

30. Ibid., 95–96.

31. Ibid., 88.

32. Ibid., 94.

33. Ibid.

34. Jacques Lacan, "Kant with Sade," trans. James B. Swenson, Jr., *October* 51 (Winter 1989) 56.

35. Ibid., 57.

36. "*Philosophy in the Bedroom* comes eight years after the *Critique of Practical Reason*. If, after having seen that the one accords with the other, we show that it completes it, we will say that it gives the truth of the *Critique*". Lacan, "Kant with Sade," 55.

37. Immanuel Kant, "An Answer to the Question: 'What is Enlightenment?'" in *Kant: Political Writings*, ed. Hans Reiss, (New York: Cambridge University Press, 1977) 55.

38. Mary Gregor, "Translator's Introduction" in Immanuel Kant, *The Conflict of the Faculties*, (New York: Abaris, 1979) ix.

39. Kant, *The Conflict of the Faculties*, 9.

40. Ibid., 19. Italics are Kant's.

41. Cited in Hannah Arendt, *Eichmann in Jerusalem: A Report on the Banality of Evil*, rev. ed. (New York: Viking, 1965) 135–137.

42. Frederick C. Beiser, *Enlightenment, Revolution, and Romanticism: The Genesis of Modern German Political Thought 1790–1800*, (Cambridge, Mass.: Harvard University Press, 1992) 50–53.

43. Ibid., 52.

44. See John Christian Laursen, "The Subversive Kant: The Vocabulary of 'Public' and 'Publicity'" in *Political Theory* 14:4, (November 1986) 584–603.

45. Kant, *The Metaphysics of Morals*, 271.

46. Michel Foucault, "The Ethic of Care for the Self as a Practice of Freedom: An Interview with Michel Foucault on January 20, 1984," trans. J. D. Gauthier, *Philosophy and Social Criticism*, 12:2–3, (1987) 113.

47. "Power is not an evil. Power is strategic games." Ibid., 129.

48. Ibid., 131.

49. Perhaps Kant arrived at the problem of discipline so late because an entire regime of discipline was only just beginning to crystalize when he wrote the three critiques. At any rate, in

his later works we see an increased focus on the history of bodies (his anthropological writings) and on how bodies can be morally educated rather than trained to be docile (his pedagogical writings).

50. Kant, *The Conflict of the Faculties*, 175.

51. Ibid., 177.

52. Ibid., 177.

53. Immanuel Kant, "An Answer to the Question: 'What is Enlightenment?'" in *Kant: Political Writings*, ed. Hans Reiss (New York: Cambridge University Press, 1977) 54.

54. Robin May Schott, *Cognition and Eros: A Critique of the Kantian Paradigm*, (University Park: The Pennsylvania State University Press, 1993) 177.

Chapter Four

1. Immanuel Kant, "An Answer to the Question: 'What is Enlightenment?'" in *Kant: Political Writings*, ed. Hans Reiss (New York: Cambridge University Press, 1977) 54.

2. Immanuel Kant, *Critique of Practical Reason*, trans. Lewis White Beck (New York: Macmillan, 1956) 20.

3. Immanuel Kant, *Grounding for the Metaphysics of Morals*, trans. James W. Ellington, (Indianapolis: Hackett Publishing Company, 1981) 8–9.

4. Robin May Schott provides an excellent discussion of Kant's castigation of desire in *Cognition and Eros: A Critique of the Kantian Paradigm* (University Park: The Pennsylvania University Press, 1993).

5. Antonin Artaud, "To Have Done with the Judgment of God" in *Antonin Artaud: Selected Writings*, ed. Susan Sontag, (New York: Farrar, Straus, and Giroux, 1976) 571.

6. Gilles Deleuze and Félix Guattari, *A Thousand Plateaus: Capitalism and Schizophrenia*, trans. Brian Massumi (Minneapolis: University of Minnesota Press, 1987) 152.

7. Ibid., 157.

8. "*Training axiom—destroy the instinctive forces in order to replace them with transmitted forces.*" Ibid., 155.

9. Cited in Schott, *Cognition and Eros*, 139.

10. Gilles Deleuze, *The Logic of Sense*, trans. Mark Lester, ed. Constantin V. Boundas, (New York: Columbia University Press, 1990), 4–5. Italics added.

11. Immanuel Kant, *Critique of Pure Reason*, trans. Norman Kemp Smith (New York: St. Martin's, 1965) A32/B49–A34/B50.

12. Gilles Deleuze, *Kant's Critical Philosophy: The Doctrine of the Faculties*, trans. Hugh Tomlinson and Barbara Hobberjam (Minneapolis: University of Minnesota Press, 1984) vii.

13. Ibid., x.

14. De Quincey, "The Last Days of Immanuel Kant," p. 177.

15. Wasianski, "Immanuel Kant in seinen letzten Lebensjahren," p. 227.

16. Thomas De Quincey, "The Last Days of Immanuel Kant" in the English Mail-Coach and Other Essays (New York: Dutton, 1961) 177.

17. J. H. W. Stuckenberg, *The Life of Immanuel Kant*, (New York: University Press of America, 1986) 160.

18. Ibid., 162.

19. De Quincey, "The Last Days of Immanuel Kant," 183.

20. Kant, in effect, constructs a unified sole-machine for his foot in the same way that he constructs a unified soul-machine for his head.

21. De Quincey, "The Last Days of Immanuel Kant," 192.

22. Ibid., 193.

23. "*Es sollte der Kaffee auf der Stelle (ein ihm gewöhnlicher Ausdruck) geschafft werden.*" E. A. Ch. Wasianski, "Immanuel Kant *in seinen letzten Lebensjahren*" in ed. Siegfried Drescher, *Wer War Kant?* (Tübingen: Neske, 1974) 237.

24. De Quincey, "The Last Days of Immanuel Kant," 182.

25. Wasianski, "Immanuel Kant *in seinen letzten Lebensjahren*," 238.

26. Deleuze, *The Logic of Sense*, 3.

27. Wasianski, "Immanuel Kant *in seinen letzten Lebensjahren*," p. 238.

28. De Quincey, "The Last Days of Immanuel Kant," 195.

29. Ibid., 201.

30. Ibid., 174–175.

31. Gregor Samsa goes to sleep a human and wakes up a vermin; Kant goes to sleep a silk-worm but wakes up a being that is human-all-to-human and, thus, in need of constant disciplining.

32. De Quincey, "The Last Days of Immanuel Kant," 175.

33. Ibid., 175. In the account given by Kant's friend Wasianski (upon which De Quincey's version is largely based). "*Wenn ich mich so ins Bett gelegt habe, so frage ich mich selbst: 'kann ein Mensch gesunder sein, als ich?*" Wasianski, "Immanuel Kant *in seinen letzten Lebensjahren*," 225.

34. Frederich Nietzsche, *Thus Spoke Zarathustra*, trans. and ed. Walter Kaufmann, *The Portable Nietzsche* (New York: Penguin, 1982) 140–142.

35. Here we might be reminded of Freud's observation that we allow ourselves to dream only when our ability to move our bodies has been turned off for the night.

36. "I openly confess [why *confess?*] that my remembering David Hume was the very thing which many years ago first interrupted my dogmatic slumber and gave my investigations in the field of speculative philosophy a quite new direction." Immanuel Kant, *Prolegomena to Any Future Metaphysics That Will Be Able to Come Forward as Science*, rev. trans. James W. Ellington (Indianapolis: Hackett, 1977) 5.

37. Gilles Deleuze, *Nietzsche and Philosophy*, trans. Hugh Tomlinson (New York: Columbia University Press, 1983) 90.

38. Jacques Lacan, "Kant with Sade," trans. James B. Swenson, Jr., *October* 51 (Winter 1989) 56.

39. Jacques Lacan, *The Four Fundamental Concepts of Psycho-Analysis*, ed. Jacques-Alain Miller, trans. Alan Sheridan, (New York: W. W. Norton and Company, 1978) 275.

40. Slavoj Zizek, *The Sublime Object of Ideology*, (New York: Verso, 1989) 81.

41. Ibid., 82.

42. "If we do not make ourselves *unworthy of happiness*, by violating our duty, we can also hope to *share* in happiness." Kant, *The Metaphysics of Morals*, 271.

43. Deleuze and Guattari's notion of desire as productive parallels, of course, Foucault's notion of disciplinary power as productive.

44. Gilles Deleuze and Félix Guattari, *Anti-Oedipus: Capitalism and Schizophrenia*, trans. Robert Hurley et al. (Minneapolis: University of Minnesota Press, 1983) 25.

45. Ibid., 25.

46. Deleuze and Guattari, *A Thousand Plateaus*, 159.

47. Ibid., 502.

48. Ibid.

49. Ibid., 503.

50. "Schizophrenia is the descent of a molecular process into a black hole." Gilles Deleuze and Claire Parnet, *Dialogues*, trans. Hugh Tomlinson and Barbara Habberjam (New York: Columbia University Press, 1987) 139.

51. Ibid., 17.

52. Deleuze and Guattari, *A Thousand Plateaus*, 167.

53. The black holes represent the eyes of this face. Deleuze and Guattari seem to be thinking of Foucauldian panopticism as the figure of disciplinary control. This omits, perhaps, the figure of the ear of the confessor that becomes so important in *The History of Sexuality*. So perhaps we should give this face big ears to serve as additional black holes—giving it an appearance not unlike that of Mickey Mouse.

54. Kant, *Critique of Practical Reason*, 166.

55. Zizek, *The Sublime Object of Ideology*, 58.

Chapter Five

1. Cited in Jürgen Habermas, *The Philosophical Discourse of Modernity*, trans. Frederick Lawrence (Cambridge, Mass.: The MIT Press, 1987) 273.

2. Foucault, of course, associates an original care of the self ethic with the ancient Greeks, who lived before the emergence of disciplinary power per se. To apply such an ethic in the present would require a certain adaptation. In an age of disciplinary domination, I am arguing, a care-of-the-self ethic would require an alternative exercise of disciplinary power.

3. Replacing the central eye of the panopticon here is the central ear of the confessor. Those who exercise power need do no more than step back and listen, awaiting the prisoners' confessions. Each isolated prisoner knows that the ear of power is listening to the other's confessions. By implicating the prisoners in their own submission to disciplinary control, the ear of power turns every victim of power into a willing accomplice in the betrayal of his or her neighbor.

4. The phrase *disciplinary matrix* appears (although not in the technical sense I am giving it here) in Judith Butler, "Editor's Introduction" in Linda Singer, *Erotic Welfare: Sexual Theory and Politics in the Age of Epidemic*, eds. Judith Butler and Maureen MacGrogan (New York: Routledge, 1993) 6. A rather different use of *disciplinary matrices* appears in Richard J. Bernstein, *Beyond Objectivism and Relativism: Science, Hermeneutics, and Praxis* (Philadelphia: University of Pennsylvania Press, 1988) x.

5. Morton D. Davis, *Game Theory: A Nontechnical Introduction* (New York: Basic Books, 1970) 101.

6. In this same sense, Gandhian Satyagraha presents itself as a paradigm for a discipline of resistance that cannot fail to win. Whether the Satyagrahis were beaten, imprisoned, or killed, they refused to act violently. As did the prisoner who cooperates, they resolutely fought for a community of resistance no matter what others did. True to their discipline of resistance, the Satyagrahis "won" precisely by refusing to become accomplices of a disciplinary matrix.

7. Kant, *The Conflict of the Faculties*, 145.

8. Freud, of course, makes this argument in *Civilization and its Discontents*, and it is critiqued by Erich Fromm in *Escape from Freedom*. Sigmund Freud, *Civilization and its Discontents*, trans. James Strachey (New York: W. W. Norton and Company, 1961) 59–63; Erich Fromm, *Escape from Freedom* (New York: Avon, 1965) 24–29. Deleuze and Guattari's critique of the Lacanian theory of desire

is also related to this question of the possibility of attaining a *summum bonum* for humanity.

9. Michel Foucault, "What is Enlightenment?" in *The Foucault Reader*, ed. Paul Rabinow (New York: Pantheon, 1984) 39.

10. Ibid., 42.

11. See, for example, Foucault's analysis of the construction of "the soul" as "the prison of the body." Michel Foucault, *Discipline and Punish: The Birth of the Prison*, trans. Alan Sheridan (New York: Vintage, 1979) 30.

12. In the trajectory of Foucault's work, we do seem to see an increasing sense of the importance of the training of reason to the training of bodies—for instance, where Foucault highlights how "we Victorians" have been trained to think about our sexuality.

13. Cited in Paul Rabinow's, "Introduction" to *The Foucault Reader* (New York: Pantheon, 1984) 13.

14. Michel Foucault, *Madness and Civilization: A History of Insanity in the Age of Reason*, trans. Richard Howard, (New York: Vintage, 1973).

15. Habermas, *The Philosophical Discourse of Modernity*, 265.

16. Ibid., 263.

17. Michel Foucault, *Power/Knowledge: Selected Interviews and Other Writings 1972–1977*, ed. Colin Gordon, trans. Colin Gordon et al. (New York: Pantheon, 1980) 133.

18. Samuel J. Todes, "Knowledge and the Ego: Kant's Three Stages of Self-Evidence" in *Kant: A Collection of Critical Essays*, ed. Robert Paul Wolff (New York: Anchor, 1967) 170–171.

19. Mark Poster, "Foucault, the Present, and History" in *Michel Foucault Philosopher*, ed. Timothy J. Armstrong (New York: Routledge, 1992) 306.

20. Gilles Deleuze, *Différence et Répétition*, (Paris: Presses Universitaires de France, 1981) 186.

21. Ronald Bogue, *Deleuze and Guattari*, (New York: Routledge, 1989) 58.

22. "We are not surprised that in *The Archaeology of Knowledge* the visible is now more or less designated only negatively, as the

nondiscursive, but that the discursive has even more discursive relations with the nondiscursive." Gilles Deleuze, *Foucault*, trans. Seán Hand, (Minneapolis: University of Minnesota Press, 1988), 67.

23. "Between the visible and the articulable we must maintain all the following aspects at the same time: the heterogeneity of the two forms, their difference in nature or anisomorphism; a mutual presupposition between the two, a mutual grappling and capture; the well-determined primacy of the one over the other." Ibid., 67–68.

24. Ibid., 68.

25. Ibid.

26. Ibid., 82.

27. Thinking the transcendental as having a history suggests the possibility of reworking Hegelian and Heideggerian themes from a Foucauldian standpoint—a future project perhaps.

Chapter Six

1. John McCumber discusses the problematic of situated freedom in *Poetic Interaction*, and my thinking has benefited from his ideas. I differ from McCumber, however in my view that transcendental limits can be construed as contingent parameters. John McCumber, *Poetic Interaction: Language, Freedom, Reason* (Chicago: The University of Chicago Press, 1989).

2. See, for example, John Rawls, *A Theory of Justice* (Cambridge: Harvard University Press, 1971) 252–254.

3. Jean-Francois Lyotard, *The Postmodern Condition: A Report on Knowledge*, trans. Geoff Bennington and Brian Massumi (Minneapolis: University of Minnesota Press, 1989) 10.

4. It is somewhat ironic that Kant's situation-sensitive critics typically bring up historically stable—and thus desituated—examples that constitute game-theoretic rather than disciplinary matrix problems.

5. See, for instance, John Rawls, "Themes in Kant's Moral Philosophy," in *Kant's Transcendental Deductions*, ed. Eckart Förster (Stanford: Stanford University Press, 1989) 81–113.

6. In suggesting that Kant give us no room to consider how broadly or narrowly to construct our maxims, I am disagreeing with the reading of Sally Sedgwick. While I certainly prefer Sedgwick's version of Kant to the stricter interpretation, Kant's absolute argument against ever lying would seem to support the latter. See Sally Sedgwick, "Can Kant's Ethics Survive the Feminist Critique?," *Pacific Philosophical Quarterly* 71 (1990) 64ff.

7. Immanuel Kant, *Critique of Practical Reason*, trans. Lewis White Beck (New York: MacMillan, 1956) 16.

8. Ibid., 15.

9. Lewis White Beck, *A Commentary on Kant's Critique of Practical Reason* (Chicago: The University of Chicago Press, 1963) 78.

10. Ibid., 81.

11. Ibid., 82.

12. Ibid., 37.

13. Martin Heidegger, *Kant and the Problem of Metaphysics*, trans. Richard Taft (Bloomington: Indiana University Press, 1990) 111.

14. Ibid., 113.

15. William Styron, *Sophie's Choice* (New York: Bantam, 1982).

16. See, for example, Friedrich Nietzsche, *Beyond Good and Evil: Prelude to a Philosophy of the Future*, trans. Walter Kaufmann (New York: Vintage, 1989) 99–100.

17. Gilles Deleuze, *Nietzsche and Philosophy*, trans. Hugh Tomlinson (New York: Columbia University Press, 1983) 68.

18. Gilles Deleuze and Félix Guattari, *A Thousand Plateaus: Capitalism and Schizophrenia*, trans. Hugh Tomlinson and Barbara Habberjam (New York: Columbia University Press, 1987) 24.

19. Michel Foucault, "Preface" in Deleuze and Guattari *Anti-Oedipus: Capitalism and Schizophrenia*, trans. Robert Hurley et al. (Minneapolis: University of Minnesota Press, 1983) xiii. Italics added.

20. Ibid., xiii–xiv.

Chapter Seven

1. Carol Gilligan, *In a Different Voice: Psychological Theory and Women's Development* (Cambridge: Harvard University Press, 1982).

2. For a good summary of this debate, see John Deigh, "Impartiality: A Closing Note," *Ethics* 101 (July 1991) 858–864.

3. For an attempt to think through the conditions under which partiality would be justified, see Marilyn Friedman, "The Practice of Partiality," *Ethics* 101 (July 1991) 818–835.

4. For a thorough discussion of this topic, see Sedwick, "Can Kant's Ethics Survive the Feminist Critique?" in *Pacific Philisophical Quarterly* 71 (1990) especially 72–76.

5. Seyla Benhabib, "In the Shadow of Aristotle and Hegel: Communicative Ethics and Current Controversies in Practical Philosophy," *The Philosophical Forum* 21:1–2, (Fall-Winter 1989–1990) 20.

6. See Herbert Marcuse, *Eros and Civilization: A Philosophical Inquiry into Freud* (Boston: Beacon Press, 1974).

7. Building on Lacanian rather than Foucauldian themes, Slavoj Zizek offers a similar argument. Slavoj Zizek, *For They Know Not What They Do: Enjoyment as a Political Factor* (New York: Verso, 1991).

8. Sandra Lee Bartky, *Femininity and Domination: Studies in the Phenomenology of Oppression* (New York: Routledge, 1990) 46ff. At issue in the debate between those who defend S&M practices as liberating versus those who reject this view is, precisely, a question of whether the "discipline" of S&M is a discipline of resistance or a discipline of domination.

9. See, for example, Harry Van Der Linden, *Kantian Ethics and Socialism* (Indianapolis: Hackett, 1988).

10. Luce Irigaray, *Speculum of the Other Woman*, trans. Gillian C. Gill (Ithaca: Cornell University Press, 1985) 204.

11. Ibid., 204.

12. Ibid., 212.

13. Née Reuter. She is called Anna Regina Reuter in Martha Lee Osborne, "Immanuel Kant" in *Woman in Western Thought*, ed. Martha Lee Osborne (New York: Random House, 1979) 153.

14. J. H. W. Stuckenberg, *The Life of Immanuel Kant* (New York: University Press of America) 167.

15. Ibid., 165.

16. "Both sexes must be educated and disciplined. Men need the former for society more than women do." Immanuel Kant, "Pedagogical Fragments" in *Kant's Educational Theory*, ed. Martin G. Brumbaugh (Philadelphia: J. B. Lippincott, 1904) 226.

17. Ibid.

18. Ibid.

19. Immanuel Kant, "Observations on the Feeling of the Beautiful and Sublime" in *Woman in Western Thought*, ed. Martha Lee Osborne (New York: Random House, 1979) 154–155.

20. Immanuel Kant, "Observations on the Feeling of the Beautiful and Sublime" in *Woman in Western Thought*, ed. Martha Lee Osborne (New York: Random House, 1979) 155. Italics added.

21. Ibid., 156. Italics added.

22. Immanuel Kant, *Lectures on Ethics*, trans. Louis Infield and J. MacMurray, (London: Methuen, 1930) 170.

23. Immanuel Kant, "Perpetual Peace: A Philosophical Sketch" in *Kant: Political Writings*, ed. Hans Reiss (New York: Cambridge University Press, 1977) 94.

24. Azar Gat, *The Origins of Military Thought: From the Enlightenment to Clausewitz* (Oxford: Clarendon Press, 1989) 79–83.

25. Immanuel Kant, *Education*, (Ann Arbor: University of Michigan Press, 1960) 2.

26. Kant, "Pedagogical Fragments," 226–227.

27. Immanuel Kant, *Anthropology from a Pragmatic Point of View*, trans. Mary Gregor (The Hague: Martinus Nijhoff, 1974), p. 171.

28. Stuckenberg, *The Life of Immanuel Kant*, 165.

29. Ibid., 431.

30. Kant, *Lectures on Ethics*, 170.

31. Irigaray, *Speculum of the Other Woman*, 204.

32. Ibid., 211. Italics omitted.

33. John George Cant's (Kant's father) "strict morality seems to have been the most striking trait of his character. He was industrious and conscientious, and was specially intent on training his children to habits of industry and to the formation of an upright character." Stuckenberg, *The Life of Immanuel Kant*, 5–6. Kant would later associate discipline with inculcating an upright character in the literal sense of an "upright gait." Kant, "Pedagogical Fragments," 225.

34. Stuckenberg, *The Life of Immanuel Kant*, 6.

35. Ibid., 7–8.

36. Ibid., 7.

37. Kant, *Critique of Pure Reason*, trans. Norman Kemp Smith (New York: St. Martin's, 1965) A141/B180–A142/B181.

Chapter Eight

1. "Almost always the men who achieve these fundamental inventions of a new paradigm have been either very young or very new to the field whose paradigm they change. And perhaps that point need not have been made explicit, for obviously these are the men who, being little committed by prior practice to the traditional rules of normal science, are particularly likely to see that those rules no longer define a playable game and to conceive another set that can replace them." Thomas S. Kuhn, *The Structure of Scientific Revolutions*, 2d ed. (Chicago: University of Chicago Press, 1970) 90.

2. Michel Foucault, *Discipline and Punish: The Birth of the Prison*, trans. Alan Sheridan (New York: Vintage, 1979) 186.

3. Ibid., 172.

4. Ibid., 168–169.

5. "The conceptual apparatus determines the senses, even before perception occurs; *a priori*, the citizen sees the world as the matter from which he himself manufactures it. Intuitively, Kant foretold what Hollywood consciously put into practice: in the very process of production, images are pre-censored according to the norm of the understanding which will later govern their apprehension." Max Horkheimer and Theodor W. Adorno, *Dialectic of Enlightenment* (New York: Continuum, 1991) 84.

6. Immanuel Kant, *The Conflict of the Faculties*, 43.

7. "Kant develops a juridical basis for the resolution of intrauniversity conflicts, and of conflicts between the university and the state, with the state serving at once as the professor's patron and censor." Richard Rand, "Preface," *Logomachia: The Conflict of the Faculties*, ed. Richard Rand (Lincoln: University of Nebraska Press, 1992) vii.

8. Kant, *Critique of Pure Reason*, A760/B788.

9. Ibid., A761/B789.

10. Ibid., A711/B739.

11. Yet at the same time, Kant views the transcendental illusions of reason as ineradicable, thus suggesting the need for a perpetual disciplining of reason.

12. Kant, *The Conflict of the Faculties*, 45.

13. Ibid., 145.

14. Jacques Derrida, "Languages and Institutions of Philosophy," *Recherches Sémiotiques/Semiotic Inquiry* Vol. 4 No. 2, (June 1984) 127.

15. Jacques Derrida, "Languages and Institutions of Philosophy," *Recherches Sémiotiques/Semiotic Inquiry*, 4:2 (June 1984) 128.

16. Kant, *The Conflict of the Faculties*, 59.

17. It was the adoption of the Kantian juridical model that led philosophers to assume the roles which we saw Habermas describing as those of usher and judge.

18. For a brief sketch of the history of the discipline of philosophy since Kant, see Richard Rorty, *Philosophy and the Mirror of Nature* (Princeton, N.J.: Princeton University Press, 1979) 3–6.

19. Alison Brown and I are presently working on a book that will undertake a study of the history and politics of the discipline of philosophy since Kant.

20. Roland Barthes, *Image, Music, Text*, trans. Stephen Heath (New York: Hill and Wang, 1977) 155.

21. Derrida, "Languages and Institutions of Philosophy," 144.

22. Ibid., 141.

23. Ibid., 146.

24. Ibid., 148.

25. Ibid.

26. Ibid., 150.

27. See also Jean Baudrillard's account of how one can end up proving pedagogy by antipedagogy. Jean Baudrillard, *Simulations*, trans. Paul Foss et al. (New York: Semiotext(e), 1983) 36.

28. According to Derrida, the regulating idea of the Collège is "to organise research on objects—themes, which are not sufficiently represented in existing institutions in France or outside France." Jacques Derrida and Geoff Bennington, "On Colleges and Philosophy" in *Postmodernism: ICA Documents 4*, ed. Lisa Appignanesi (London: Free Association Books, 1989) 210.

29. "Within the Collège, we are interested, among other things, in the history and the structure of the philosophical institution as such, and of philosophical teaching as such." Ibid., 211.

30. Ibid., 213.

31. Ibid. Italics added.

32. Elsewhere, Derrida speaks of "the necessity for a new way of educating students that will prepare them to undertake new analyses," and of "preparing oneself . . . to transform the modes of writing, approaches to pedagogy, the procedures of academic exchange, the relation to the languages, to other disciplines, to the institution in general." Jacques Derrida, "The Principle of Reason: The University in the Eyes of its Pupils," *Diacritics* 13:33 (Fall 1983) 16–17.

33. Jacques Derrida, "Mochlos" in Rand, ed., *Logomachia: The Conflict of the Faculties* (Lincoln: University of Nebraska Press, 1992) especially 13–15.

34. Michel Foucault, *The Archaeology of Knowledge and the Discourse on Language*, trans. A. M. Sheridan Smith (New York: Pantheon Books, 1972) 222.

35. Ibid., 223.

36. Rorty, *Philosophy and the Mirror of Nature*, 370.

37. "Some of us have argued in recent years for a politically active role for philosophers, holding that we should take stands

on matters of public policy and perhaps even take actions, *as philosophers*, and through our professional organizations, not just as private citizens. This approach has not, to put it mildly, swept through the profession." Virginia Held, *Rights and Goods: Justifying Social Action* (Chicago: The University of Chicago Press, 1984), 10. Italics are Held's.

38. The phrase is from Herbert Marcuse, *One-Dimensional Man* (Boston: Beacon Press, 1966) 1.

Bibliography

Arendt, Hannah *Eichmann in Jerusalem: A Report on the Banality of Evil*, rev. ed. (New York: Viking, 1965).

Armstrong, Timothy J., ed. *Michel Foucault Philosopher* (New York: Routledge, 1992).

Artaud, Antonin "To Have Done with the Judgment of God" in *Antonin Artaud: Selected Writings*, ed. Susan Sontag (New York: Farrar, Straus, and Giroux, 1976).

Barthes, Roland. *Image, Music, Text*, trans. Stephen Heath (New York: Hill and Wang, 1977).

Bartky, Sandra Lee. *Femininity and Domination: Studies in the Phenomenology of Oppression* (New York: Routledge, 1990).

Baudrillard, Jean. *Simulations*, trans. Paul Foss et al. (New York: Semiotext(e), 1983).

Beck, Lewis White. *A Commentary on Kant's Critique of Practical Reason* (Chicago: The University of Chicago Press, 1963).

Beiser, Frederick C. *Enlightenment, Revolution, and Romanticism: The Genesis of Modern German Political Thought 1790–1800*, (Cambridge, Mass.: Harvard University Press, 1992).

Benhabib, Seyla. "In the Shadow of Aristotle and Hegel: Communicative Ethics and Current Controversies in Practical Philosophy," *The Philosophical Forum* 21:1–2, (Fall-Winter 1989–1990).

Bernstein, Richard J. *Beyond Objectivism and Relativism: Science, Hermeneutics, and Praxis* (Philadelphia: University of Pennsylvania Press, 1988).

———. "Foucault: Critique as a Philosophical Ethos" in *Philosophical Interventions in the Unfinished Project of Enlightenment*, ed. Axel Honneth et al. (Cambridge, Mass.: The MIT Press, 1992).

———. *The New Constellation* (Cambridge, Mass.: The MIT Press, 1992).

Bogue, Ronald. *Deleuze and Guattari* (New York: Routledge, 1989).

Butler, Judith. "Editor's Introduction" in Linda Singer, *Erotic Welfare: Sexual Theory and Politics in the Age of Epidemic*, eds. Judith Butler and Maureen MacGrogan (New York: Routledge, 1993).

Davis, Morton D. *Game Theory: A Nontechnical Introduction* (New York: Basic Books, 1970).

Deigh, John. "Impartiality: A Closing Note," *Ethics* 101 (July 1991) 858–864.

Deleuze, Gilles. *Présentation de Sacher-Masoch*, (Paris: *Les éditions de Minuit*, 1967).

———. *Différence et Répétition* (Paris: Presses Universitaires de France, 1981).

———. *Nietzsche and Philosophy*, trans. Hugh Tomlinson (New York: Columbia University Press, 1983).

———. *Kant's Critical Philosophy: The Doctrine of the Faculties*, trans. Hugh Tomlinson and Barbara Habberjam (Minneapolis: University of Minnesota Press, 1984).

———. *Foucault*, trans. Seán Hand (Minneapolis: University of Minnesota Press, 1988).

———. *The Logic of Sense*, trans. Mark Lester, ed. Constantin V. Boundas (New York: Columbia University Press, 1990).

Deleuze, Gilles, and Félix Guattari. *Anti-Oedipus: Capitalism and Schizophrenia*, trans. Robert Hurley et al. (Minneapolis: University of Minnesota Press, 1983).

———. *A Thousand Plateaus: Capitalism and Schizophrenia*, trans. Brian Massumi (Minneapolis: University of Minnesota Press, 1987).

Deleuze, Gilles, and Claire Parnet. *Dialogues*, trans. Hugh Tomlinson and Barbara Habberjam (New York: Columbia University Press, 1987).

De Quincey, Thomas, "The Last Days of Immanuel Kant" in *The English Mail-Coach and Other Essays* (New York: Dutton, 1961).

Derridan, Jacques. "The Principle of Reason: The University in the Eyes of its Pupils," *Diacritics* 13:33 (Fall 1983).

———. "Languages and Institutions of Philosophy," *Recherches Sémiotiques/Semiotic Inquiry* 4:2, (June 1984).

———. "Mochlos; Or The Conflict of the Faculties" in *Logomachia: The Conflict of the Faculties*, ed. Richard Rand (Lincoln: University of Nebraska Press, 1992).

Derrida, Jacques, and Geoff Bennington. "On Colleges and Philosophy" in *Postmodernism: ICA Documents 4*, ed. Lisa Appignanesi (London: Free Association Books, 1989).

Drescher, Siegfried, ed. *Wer War Kant?* (Tübingen: Neske, 1974).

Förster, Eckart, ed. *Kant's Transcendental Deductions* (Stanford: Stanford Calif.: University Press, 1989).

Foucault, Michel. *The Archaeology of Knowledge and the Discourse on Language*, trans. A. M. Sheridan Smith (New York: Pantheon Books, 1972).

———. *Madness and Civilization: A History of Insanity in the Age of Reason*, trans. Richard Howard (New York: Vintage, 1973).

———. *Discipline and Punish: The Birth of the Prison*, trans. Alan Sheridan (New York: Vintage, 1979).

———. *Power/Knowledge: Selected Interviews and Other Writings 1972–1977*, ed. Colin Gordon, trans. Colin Gordon et al. (New York: Pantheon, 1980).

———. "Two Lectures," op.cit.

———. "Preface" in Gilles Deleuze and Félix Guattari, *Anti-Oedipus: Capitalization and Schizophrenia*, trans. Robert Hurley et al. (Minneapolis: University of Minnesota Press, 1983).

———. "What is Enlightenment?" in *The Foucault Reader*, ed. Paul Rabinow (New York: Pantheon, 1984).

———. "The Ethic of Care for the Self as a Practice of Freedom: An Interview with Michel Foucault on January 20, 1984," trans. J. D. Gauthier, *Philosophy and Social Criticism* 12:2–3, (1987).

———. *The Care of the Self: Vol. 3, The History of Sexuality*, trans. Robert Hurley (New York: Vintage, 1988).

———. *Foucault Live: (Interviews, 1966–1984)* (New York: Semiotext(e), 1989).

———. *An Introduction, vol. 1, The History of Sexuality*, trans. Robert Hurley (New York: Vintage, 1990).

Fraser, Nancy *Unruly Practices: Power, Discourse, and Gender in Contemporary Social Theory* (Minneapolis: University of Minnesota Press, 1989).

Friedman, Marilyn. "The Practice of Partiality," *Ethics* 101 (July 1991) 818–835.

Freud, Sigmund. *Civilization and Its Discontents*, trans. James Strachey (New York: W. W. Norton and Company, 1961).

Fromm, Erich. *Escape from Freedom* (New York: Avon, 1965).

Gat, Azar *The Origins of Military Thought: From the Enlightenment to Clausewitz* (Oxford: Clarendon Press, 1989).

Gilligan, Carol *In a Different Voice: Psychological Theory and Women's Development* (Cambridge, Mass.: Harvard University Press, 1982).

Gregor, Mary. "Translator's Introduction" in Immanuel Kant, *The Conflict of the Faculties* (New York: Abaris, 1979).

Habermas, Jürgen. *Knowledge and Human Interests*, trans. Jeremy J. Shapiro (Boston: Beacon, 1971).

——. *The Philosophical Discourse of Modernity*, trans. Frederick Lawrence (Cambridge, Mass.: The MIT Press, 1987).

——. "Philosophy as Stand-In and Interpreter," in *After Philosophy: End or Transformation*, ed. Kenneth Baynes et al. (Cambridge, Mass.: The MIT Press, 1987).

Hegel, G. W. F. *Phenomenology of Spirit*, trans. A.V. Miller (New York: Oxford University Press, 1977).

Heidegger, Martin. *Being and Time*, trans. John Macquarrie and Edward Robinson (New York: Harper and Row, 1962).

——. *Kant and the Problem of Metaphysics*, trans. Richard Taft (Bloomington: Indiana University Press, 1990).

Held, Virginia. *Rights and Goods: Justifying Social Action* (Chicago: The University of Chicago Press, 1984).

Henrich, Dieter. "Kant's Notion of a Deduction and the Methodological Background of the First *Critique*" in *Kant's Transcendental Deductions*, ed. Eckart Förster (Stanford, Calif.: Stanford University Press, 1989).

Horkheimer, Max, and Theodor W. Adorno. *Dialectic of Enlightenment* (New York: Continuum, 1991).

Hoy, David Couzens. "Introduction" in *Foucault: A Critical Reader*, ed. David Couzens Hoy (New York: Blackwell, 1986).

Irigaray, Luce. *Speculum of the Other Woman*, trans. Gillian C. Gill (Ithaca: Cornell University Press, 1985).

Jachmann, Reinhold Bernhard. "Immanuel Kant *geschildert in Briefen an einen Freund*" in ed. Siegfried Drescher, *Wer War Kant?* (Tübingen: Neske, 1974).

Kant, Immanuel. "Pedagogical Fragments" in *Kant's Educational Theory*, ed. Martin G. Brumbaugh (Philadelphia: J. B. Lippincott Company, 1904).

————. *Lectures on Ethics*, trans. Louis Infield and J. MacMurray (London: Methuen, 1930).

————. *Critique of Practical Reason*, trans. Lewis White Beck (New York: Macmillan, 1956).

————. *Education* (Ann Arbor: University of Michigan Press, 1960).

————. *Critique of Pure Reason*, trans. Norman Kemp Smith (New York: St. Martin's, 1965).

————. *Anthropology from a Pragmatic Point of View*, trans. Mary Gregor (The Hague: Martinus Nijhoff, 1974).

————. *Kant: Political Writings*, ed. Hans Reiss (New York: Cambridge University Press, 1977).

————. "An Answer to the Question: 'What is Enlightenment?'" op.cit.

————. "Idea for a Universal History with a Cosmopolitan Purpose," op.cit.

————. "Perpetual Peace: A Philosophical Sketch," op.cit.

————. *Prolegomena to Any Future Metaphysics That Will Be Able to Come Forward as Science*, rev. trans. James W. Ellington (Indianapolis: Hackett, 1977).

————. "Observations on the Feeling of the Beautiful and Sublime" in *Woman in Western Thought*, ed. Martha Lee Osborne (New York: Random House, 1979).

------. *Grounding for the Metaphysics of Morals*, trans. James W. Ellington (Indianapolis: Hackett Publishing Company, 1981).

------. *The Metaphysics of Morals*, trans. Mary Gregor (New York: Cambridge University Press, 1991).

Kortian, Garbis. *Metacritique: The Philosophical Argument of Jürgen Habermas*, trans. John Raffan (New York: Cambridge University Press, 1980).

Kuhn, Thomas S. *The Structure of Scientific Revolutions*, 2d ed. (Chicago: University of Chicago Press, 1970).

Lacan, Jacques. *The Four Fundamental Concepts of Psycho-Analysis*, ed. Jacques-Alain Miller, trans. Alan Sheridan (New York: W. W. Norton and Company, 1978).

------. "Kant with Sade," trans. James B. Swenson, Jr., *October* 51 (Winter 1989).

Laursen, John Christian. "The Subversive Kant: The Vocabulary of 'Public' and 'Publicity,'" *Political Theory* 14:4 (November 1986).

Lyotard, Jean-François. *The Postmodern Condition: A Report on Knowledge*, trans. Geoff Bennington and Brian Massumi (Minneapolis: University of Minnesota Press, 1989).

Marcuse, Herbert. *One-Dimensional Man* (Boston: Beacon Press, 1966).

------. *Eros and Civilization: A Philosophical Inquiry into Freud* (Boston: Beacon Press, 1974).

Massumi, Brian. "Translator's Foreword" in Gilles Deleuze and Félix Guattari, *A Thousand Plateaus: Capitalism and Schizophrenia*, trans. Robert Hurley et al. (Minneapolis: University of Minnesota Press, 1983).

McCumber, John. *Poetic Interaction: Language, Freedom, Reason* (Chicago: The University of Chicago Press, 1989).

------. *The Company of Words* (Evanston, Ill.: Northwestern University Press, 1993).

Moi, Toril. *Sexual/Textual Politics: Feminist Literary Theory*, (New York: Routledge, 1988).

Nietzsche, Friedrich. *Thus Spoke Zarathustra* in *The Portable Nietzsche*, trans. and ed. Walter Kaufmann (New York: Penguin, 1982).

———. *Beyond Good and Evil: Prelude to a Philosophy of the Future*, trans. Walter Kaufmann (New York: Vintage, 1989).

Osborne, Martha Lee. "Immanuel Kant" in *Woman in Western Thought*, ed. Martha Lee Osborne (New York: Random House, 1979).

Poster, Mark. "Foucault, the Present, and History" in *Michel Foucault Philosopher*, ed. Timothy J. Armstrong (New York: Routledge, 1992).

Rand, Richard, ed. *Logomachia: The Conflict of the Faculties* (Lincoln: University of Nebraska Press, 1992).

Rawls, John. *A Theory of Justice* (Cambridge: Harvard University Press, 1971).

———. "Themes in Kant's Moral Philosophy," in *Kant's Transcendental Deductions*, ed. Eckart Förster (Stanford, Calif.: Stanford University Press, 1989).

Rochlitz, Rainer. "The Aesthetics of Existence: Post-Conventional Morality and the Theory of Power in Michel Foucault" in *Michel Foucault Philosopher*, ed. Timothy J. Armstrong (New York: Routledge Press, 1992).

Rorty, Richard *Philosophy and the Mirror of Nature* (Princeton, N.J.: Princeton University Press, 1979).

Rose, Gillian *Dialectic of Nihilism: Post-Structuralism and Law* (New York: Basil Blackwell, 1984).

Schott, Robin May. *Cognition and Eros: A Critique of the Kantian Paradigm* (University Park: The Pennsylvania State University Press, 1993).

Schürmann, Reiner. *Heidegger on Being and Acting: From Principles to Anarchy*, trans. Christine-Marie Gros (Bloomington: Indiana University Press, 1987).

Sedwick, Sally. "Can Kant's Ethics Survive the Feminist Critique?," *Pacific Philosophical Quarterly* 71 (1990). 60–79

Stuckenberg, J. H. W. *The Life of Immanuel Kant* (New York: University Press of America, 1986).

Styron, William. *Sophie's Choice* (New York: Bantam, 1982).

Todes, Samuel J. "Knowledge and the Ego: Kant's Three Stages of Self-Evidence" in *Kant: A Collection of Critical Essays*, ed. Robert Paul Wolff (New York: Anchor, 1967).

Van Der Linden, Harry. *Kantian Ethics and Socialism* (Indianapolis: Hackett, 1988).

Wasianski, E. A. Ch. "Immanuel Kant *in seinen letzten Lebensjahren*" in *Wer War Kant?*, ed. Siegfried Drescher (Tübingen: Neske, 1974).

Winfield, Richard Dien. *Overcoming Foundations: Studies in Systematic Philosophy* (New York: Columbia University Press, 1989).

Žižek, Slavoj. *The Sublime Object of Ideology* (New York: Verso, 1989).

———. *For They Know Not What They Do: Enjoyment as a Political Factor* (New York: Verso, 1991).

Index of Names